"People don't take trips—
trips take people."

John Steinbeck, the writer who first inspired
WILDSAM, wrote those words in his American
epic *Travels with Charley*. They capture the core
belief of the book you now hold in your hands:
That unforgettable experiences are born from the
unexpected. And road trips, most especially, beg the
traveler to write plans in pencil and trace routes
on the fly. May the stories in these pages stoke
this kind of adventure.

WILDSAM
FIELD GUIDES

Our sincere appreciation to the Atlanta
History Museum, Southern Foodways Alliance,
Birmingham Civil Rights Institute, *Atlanta
Journal-Constitution*, Memphis *Commercial Appeal*,
New Orleans *Times-Picayune*, Barrett Austin,
Joe York, George Jones, Scott Barretta,
Ashley Graham, Philip Lorish, Caleb Chancey,
Steve Graves, Melissa Farrell and Corey Maynard.
And to Booker and Truett: this is your other home;
we'll explore it one day together.

WILDSAM FIELD GUIDES

ISBN 978-1-5323-3511-2

Art direction by SDCO Partners
Illustrations by Jamison Harper

For more information, visit wildsam.com.

Special thanks to ProPublica for permission to reprint
Nikole Hannah-Jones' essay "Ghosts of Greenwood" in full.

# CONTENTS

*Discover the people and places that tell the story of the American South*

*There ain't no grave can hold my body down*
*There ain't no grave can hold my body down*
*When I hear that trumpet sound I'm gonna rise right out of the ground*
*Ain't no grave can hold my body down*

*Well, look way down the river, what do you think I see?*
*I see a band of angels and they're coming after me*
*Ain't no grave can hold my body down*
*There ain't no grave can hold my body down*

*Well, look down yonder Gabriel, put your feet on the land and see*
*But Gabriel don't you blow your trumpet 'til you hear it from me*
*There ain't no grave can hold my body down*
*Ain't no grave can hold my body down*

*Well, meet me Jesus, meet me. Meet me in the middle of the air*
*And if these wings don't fail me I will meet you anywhere*
*Ain't no grave can hold my body down*
*There ain't no grave can hold my body down*

*Well, meet me mother and father, meet me down the river road*
*And momma you know that I'll be there when I check my load*
*Ain't no grave can hold my body down*
*There ain't no grave can hold my body down*
*There ain't no grave can hold my body down*

*—Claude Ely,* 1934

# WELCOME

——

**ON JANUARY 26, 2017,** I picked up a *New York Times* newspaper. On the front page, below the fold, I read this headline: "White Police Chief Apologizes for a 1940 Southern Lynching." The story was about Austin Callaway, a black teenager accused of attacking a white woman, and the mob of masked men who took him from the city jail, drove him eight miles into the country and shot him. The local *Daily* in LaGrange, Georgia, gave murky details of the crime and Austin Callaway. He was either 16 or 18 years old, they wrote; it was unclear.

LaGrange, Georgia, is my hometown. It's sewn onto the banks of the Chattahoochee River, sharing a border with Alabama, where my father's roots reach deep into the earth. Until last January, I'd never heard Austin Callaway's name. Not a whisper of his murder. It was as if his story were buried with him in the unmarked grave. When I sit with Austin's story, on that day and this one, the whole thing sinks and swells inside me, a weight of lies and original sin.

The South starts here. In the unbearable tensions. Oppression and guilt. Death and life. Beauty and sorrow. Because this is my home, and these are my people, I cannot escape the two stories. They are like the two trees wrapped together on my family farm. And in the words of pioneering black journalist Ida B. Wells: "The only way to right wrongs is to turn the light of truth upon them."

In that light of truth, the South is a poem, verses that conjure magical thinking: Lowcountry, Smokies, Blue Ridge, Black Belt and Outer Banks. It is the morning sun on a Savannah square; the sizzling pans at Doe's in the Delta; fireflies blinking all at once down that Tennessee road. Darkness; then light. It is ten thousand novels and ten thousand songs, their flames flickering in lanterns, finding love in those ruins. It is a 12-year-old in Puckett's Creek, Virginia, the year 1934, the boy told that the tuberculosis is bad, that he is going to die. His uncle handing over the worn guitar, the boy bringing forth an unknown song. *There ain't no grave can hold my body down.*

It is all true. The South is a place of many graves; memory is the resurrection.    —*TB*

# ESSENTIALS

Trusted intel and
traveler info about iconic
regional culture and practices

# PLANNING

TRANSPORT

**PONTOON BOAT**
Lake Martin, Alexander City, AL
*russellmarine.net*

....................................................

**SEAPLANE**
Key West, FL
*keysseaplanes.com*

....................................................

**SHRIMP BOAT**
Darien, GA
*captgabby.com*

....................................................

**NASCAR RV**
Talladega, AL/Bristol, TN
*trinityrvrentals.com*

....................................................

**STREETCAR**
St. Charles Line, New Orleans, LA
*norta.com*

....................................................

**CANOE**
Ponca, AR
*buffaloriver.com*

....................................................

**HORSE CARRIAGE**
Charleston, SC
*palmettocarriage.com*

....................................................

**RAFTING**
Bryson City, NC
*noc.com*

....................................................

**VINTAGE CARS**
Cleveland, TN
*creekridgeclassiccar.com*

CLIMATE

Hemmed in by Gulf and Atlantic waters, the Southen states share a sultry summer, beginning when fireflies appear in late May through the rumble of thunderstorms in August. When hurricane season slows in November, winter winds bring down autumn color and, if stars align, a few inches of blessed snow.

CALENDAR

| | |
|---|---|
| JAN | 30A Songwriters Festival Seaside, FL |
| FEB | Mardi Gras New Orleans, LA |
| MAR | Shag Dance Competition Myrtle Beach, SC |
| APR | The Masters Augusta, GA |
| MAY | Wild Ramp Season Great Smoky Mts NP |
| JUN | Peak Trout Fishing White River, AR |
| JUL | Neshoba County Fair Philadelphia, MS |
| AUG | Old Fiddlers Convention Galax, VA |
| SEP | Keeneland Yearling Sale Lexington, KY |
| OCT | Lexington Barbecue Festival, Lexington, NC |
| NOV | Iron Bowl Tuscaloosa/Auburn, AL |
| DEC | Lessons and Carols Sewanee, TN |

# GEOGRAPHY

*Notable terrain formations and where to find them.*

SALT MARSHES
Spartina cordgrass covers bio-rich zone caked with pluff mud and oyster beds. *ACE Basin, SC*

CAVERNS
Long caves, deep caves, dome caves, hidden caves, sinkhole caves, caves of caves. *Neversink Pit, AL*

MOUNTAIN BALDS
Wind-swept Appalachian summits swarded in thick grasses and sedges. *Gregory Bald, NC*

LONGLEAF FORESTS
Once omnipresent, the "heart" pine covers less than 5 million U.S. acres. *Moody Forest Natural Area, GA*

BLACKWATER RIVERS
Meandering, swampy, dark tannic waters sometimes mistaken as lazy. *Saint Marys River, FL*

CYPRESS SWAMPS
Wetlands and deltas staked with the iconic, knobby-knee buttress trees. *Atchafalaya Basin, LA*

# FOODWAYS

*History, culture and tradition in a dish.*

| | |
|---|---|
| Shrimp and Grits | An amalgamation of creamy corn grits, sautéed shrimp and bacon-tomato gravy; originally a Lowcountry breakfast. *Crook's Corner, Chapel Hill, NC* |
| Fried Chicken | Battered and pan-fried yardbird anchors the Southern table. Buttermilk brine yields juicy meat. *Gus's World Famous Fried Chicken, Memphis, TN* |
| Pimiento Cheese | Mayonnaise, grated cheese and pimiento peppers served on sliced bread or crackers. *Hominy Grill, Charleston, SC* |
| Vegetable Plates | This lunch of assorted vegetables—simmered in pork fat, served fresh off the knife and baked as casseroles—champions the agrarian soul. *Miller Union, Atlanta, GA* |
| Coconut Cake | Draped in seven-minute frosting and covered in a snowdrift of coconut, popular on holiday tables. *Chez Fonfon, Birmingham, AL* |

# HISTORY

# MEDIA

FILM

*Selma*
*Coal Miner's Daughter*
*O Brother, Where Art Thou?*
*Deliverance*
*A Streetcar Named Desire*
*Hustle & Flow*
*12 Years a Slave*
*To Kill a Mockingbird*
*Forrest Gump*
*Winter's Bone*

MUSIC

Hank Williams
Mahalia Jackson
Bill Monroe and His Blue Grass Boys
Fats Domino
Jason Isbell
James Brown
Loretta Lynn
Shovels & Rope
BB King
Sam & Dave

BOOKS

☞ *Carry Me Home* by Diane McWhorter: The 700-page personal tour de force spotlights the dark terror of 1963 Birmingham, from Klan rallies to church bombings. Won the 2002 Pulitzer.

..............................................................................

☞ *Slaves in the Family* by Edward Ball: Luminous, real-life exploration into the lost narratives of the author's family's South Carolina plantation and the descendants of its slaves.

..............................................................................

☞ *The Complete Stories* by Flannery O'Connor: From "Good Country People" to "The Life You Save May Be Your Own," O'Connor captures the violent, curious, misfit and, yes, gothic South.

..............................................................................

☞ *Sing, Unburied, Sing* by Jesmyn Ward: The second of Ward's two National Book Award winners is an "odyssey" novel and family story coiled with the region's lineage of poverty and racism.

..............................................................................

☞ *Absalom, Absalom!* by William Faulkner: Civil War—era saga follows Mississippi patriarch Thomas Sutpen in a spiraling family history that helped Faulkner land the Nobel.

..............................................................................

☞ *The Sport of Kings* by C.E. Morgan: Fictional epic of a thoroughbred heir to Secretariat and the dirty ambition and haunted myths of Kentucky horse racing culture.

# LODGING

### CARRIAGE HOUSE
Zero George
*Charleston, SC*
*zerogeorge.com*
Deep porches, fancy millwork, courtyard that feels like a secret.

.........................

### COASTAL RESORT
The Cloister
*Sea Island, GA*
*seaisland.com*
Circa 1928, tony beach villa steeped in history, design lavishes.

.........................

### RETRO
Hotel Clermont
*Atlanta, GA*
*hotelclermont.com*
Funky 1924 revamp, stumbling distance from iconic Clermont Lounge.

.........................

### SPORTING LODGE
Primland
*Meadows of Dan, VA*
*primland.com*
Blue Ridge estate with luxe treehouses for guided bird hunts.

### ART HOTEL
21c Museum Hotel
*Louisville, KY*
*21cmuseumhotels.com*
Tobacco warehouse reimagined by art collectors, now seven locations.

.........................

### COUNTRY VILLA
Hotel Domestique
*Travelers Rest, SC*
*hoteldomestique.com*
Upcountry yoga and cycling retreat from local Tour de France racer.

.........................

### MODERN CITY
Quirk Hotel
*Richmond, VA*
*destinationhotels.com*
Sleek furniture and pink palette, anchors downtown design district.

.........................

### FAMILY RETREAT
High Hampton Resort
*Cashiers, NC*
*highhamptonresort.com*
Wooded wonderland with classic lodge, private lake, afternoon tea.

### FRENCH ANTIQUE
Soniat House
*New Orleans, LA*
*soniathouse.com*
Iron balcony ambiance with an honor bar and biscuits every morning.

.........................

### NEW BOUTIQUE
Noelle Hotel
*Nashville, TN*
*noelle-nashville.com*
A 224-room design love child created by Nashville's brightest artisans.

.........................

### BEACH TOWN
The Pearl
*Rosemary Beach, FL*
*thepearlrb.com*
The 55-room seafront jewel on 30A, sugary beaches minutes away.

.........................

### RUSTIC
Hike Inn
*Dawsonville, GA*
*hike-inn.com*
Backcountry respite that's only accessible by a five-mile amble on the AT.

# PARKS AND PUBLIC LANDS

*Lesser-known state and national territories*
*and the prime lookouts within.*

**TENNESSEE**
Savage Gulf Natural Area — *Greeter Falls, Stone Door, Savage Creek*
Over 15,000 acres of sandstone cliffs and underground streams, coated
in specimen hickories and yellow poplars of the Cumberland Plateau.
.................................................................

**LOUISIANA**
Chicot State Park — *8-mile Canoe Trail, State Arboretum*
Canoe paths snake through this stately cypress-tupelo swamp with a
beech-magnolia preserve for 150 Louisiana plant species.
.................................................................

**GEORGIA**
Chattahoochee National Forest — *Springer Mountain, Dukes Creek*
Vast 18-county swath with trout streams and 400 hiker miles, including
the southern terminus of the Appalachian Trail.
.................................................................

**NORTH CAROLINA**
Cape Hatteras National Seashore — *Cape Point, Okracoke Island*
Shipwreck graveyard of the Outer Banks, this 70-mile land ribbon
comprises sand dunes, salt marshes and deserted beaches.
.................................................................

**ALABAMA**
Little River Canyon — *Eberhart Point, Martha's Falls*
A 12-mile sandstone spectacle has 600-foot cliffs and mammoth
boulders bowled into the blue-green river and pristine pools below.
.................................................................

**KENTUCKY**
Red River Gorge — *The Motherlode, Sky Bridge, Sheltowee Trail*
Climber's paradise with arches and cliff overhangs upshot all over this
29,000-acre canyon system carved inside Daniel Boone National Forest.
.................................................................

**SOUTH CAROLINA**
Edisto River — *Four Holes Swamp, Botany Bay*
America's longest free-flowing blackwater river meanders through
mossy oaks and baldcypress to ACE Basin, ending at Edisto Beach.

---

# ISSUES

**Upward Mobility** — With fourth-grade reading below the national proficiency and ten states ranking among the highest 13 in poverty rates, economic mobility in the South remains lethargic, if not static.
**EXPERT:** *David Dodson, president of MDC and "State of the South" reports in Durham, NC*

**Coastal Erosion** — A doomsday scenario brought on by levee construction, rising Gulf waters and pursuits of oil and gas has left the Louisiana coastline disappearing at a rate of a football field an hour.
**EXPERT:** *Denise Reed, Laboratory for Coastal Restoration Science, University of New Orleans*

**Mass Incarceration** — Racial disparity is stark in prisons across the region. In Louisiana, black people make up 32% of the general population and 68% of its prison population; in Mississippi [37/65], South Carolina [27/65], Georgia [30/62] and Alabama [26/59].
**EXPERT:** *Michelle Alexander, author of* The New Jim Crow

**Rural Crossroads** — With seven states over 30% rural, small towns remain vital threads, while facing modern challenges like opioid addiction, reliable broadband and immigrant rights.
**EXPERT:** *Whitney Kimball Coe, coordinator of National Rural Assembly, Athens, TN*

STATISTICS

89% ............................Amount of U.S. peanut crop grown in the South
1,288 ...... Faulkner's longest sentence [in words] from *Absalom, Absalom!*
216 .... Tornadoes on April 27, 2011, during super outbreak in AL and MS
17...... James Beard Award-winning chefs from New Orleans [as of 2018]
$137,500................Price for 1939 Bill Traylor's "Drinking Man With Dog"
621 .....................Wins by John McKissick, high school football coach in Summerville, SC

## ALABAMA

**EST.** 1819  **MOTTO:** *We dare defend our rights*

..........................................................

⊕ STATE BIRD
  YELLOWHAMMER

✳ STATE FLOWER
  CAMELLIA

◈ STATE GEM
  STAR BLUE QUARTZ

♫ STATE SONG
  "ALABAMA"

SMALL FESTIVAL
Billy Reid's Shindig
*billyreid.com/
  the-shindig-archive*

..........................................................

RESTAURANT
Highlands Bar & Grill
Birmingham
*highlandsbarandgrill.com*

..........................................................

BAR
Manci's Antique Club
Daphne
*mancisantiqueclub.com*

..........................................................

SCENIC DRIVE
Lookout Mountain Parkway
*From Chattanooga to Gadsden*

..........................................................

DETOUR
Rural Studio
Newbern
*ruralstudio.org*

..........................................................

MEMENTO
DIY Sewing Kit
Alabama Chanin
*alabamachanin.com*

## ARKANSAS

**EST.** 1836  **MOTTO:** *The people rule*

..........................................................

⊕ STATE BIRD
  MOCKINGBIRD

✳ STATE FLOWER
  APPLE BLOSSOM

◈ STATE GEM
  DIAMOND

♫ STATE SONG
  "ARKANSAS (YOU RUN DEEP IN ME)"

SMALL FESTIVAL
King Biscuit Blues Festival
Helena
*kingbiscuitfestival.com*

..........................................................

RESTAURANT
McClard's Bar-B-Q
Hot Springs
*mcclards.com*

..........................................................

BAR
The White Water Tavern
Little Rock
*whitewatertavern.com*

..........................................................

SCENIC DRIVE
Scenic 7 Byway
*El Dorado to Jasper*

..........................................................

DETOUR
Thorncrown Chapel
Eureka Springs
*thorncrown.com*

..........................................................

MEMENTO
PK Grill
Little Rock
*pkgrills.com*

# FLORIDA

**EST.** 1845  **MOTTO:** *In God we trust*

.............................................

⊕ STATE BIRD
MOCKINGBIRD

✸ STATE FLOWER
ORANGE BLOSSOM

◈ STATE GEM
MOONSTONE

♫ STATE SONG
"THE SWANEE RIVER"

SMALL FESTIVAL
Florida Seafood Festival
Apalachicola
*floridaseafoodfestival.com*

.............................................

RESTAURANT
Roy's
Steinhatchee
*roys-restaurant.com*

.............................................

BAR
Bud and Alley's
Seaside
*budandalleys.com*

.............................................

SCENIC DRIVE
Highway 98
*Tallahassee to Apalachicola*

.............................................

DETOUR
Mermaids at Weeki
Wachee Springs
*weekiwachee.com*

.............................................

MEMENTO
*Saints of Old Florida* book
Joseph's Cottage
Port St. Joe

# GEORGIA

**EST.** 1788  **MOTTO:** *Wisdom, justice and moderation*

.............................................

⊕ STATE BIRD
BROWN THRASHER

✸ STATE FLOWER
CHEROKEE ROSE

◈ STATE GEM
QUARTZ

♫ STATE SONG
"GEORGIA ON MY MIND"

SMALL FESTIVAL
Blessing of the Fleet
Darien
*blessingofthefleet.com*

.............................................

RESTAURANT
Fresh Air Barbecue
Jackson
*freshairbarbecue.com*

.............................................

BAR
Ticonderoga Club
Atlanta
*ticonderogaclub.com*

.............................................

SCENIC DRIVE
Cohutta-Chattahoochee
*U.S. 41, State Route 52*

.............................................

DETOUR
Waffle House Museum
Decatur
770-326-7086

.............................................

MEMENTO
Raw Acacia Honeycomb
Savannah Bee
*savannahbee.com*

## KENTUCKY

**EST.** 1792   **STATE BIRD:** *Northern Cardinal*   **STATE FLOWER:** *Goldenrod*

......................................................................

SMALL FESTIVAL

Berea Craft Festival
Berea
*bereacraftfestival.com*

......................................................

MEMENTO

Sterling Silver Julep cups
Shelbyville
*julepcups.com*

RESTAURANT

Holly Hill Inn
Midway
*hollyhillinn.com*

.............................................

SCENIC DRIVE

Old Frankfort Pike
*Lexington to Frankfort*

## LOUISIANA

**EST.** 1812   **STATE BIRD:** *Brown Pelican*   **STATE FLOWER:** *Magnolia*

......................................................................

SMALL FESTIVAL

Wooden Boat Festival
Madisonville
*woodenboatfest.org*

..........................................

MEMENTO

Chicory coffee
Cafe Du Monde
*cafedumonde.com*

RESTAURANT

Galatoire's
New Orleans
*galatoires.com*

.............................................

SCENIC DRIVE

Hwy 90
*Breaux Bridge to New Orleans*

## MISSISSIPPI

**EST.** 1817   **STATE BIRD:** *Mockingbird*   **STATE FLOWER:** *Magnolia*

......................................................................

SMALL FESTIVAL

Delta Hot Tamale Festival
Greenville

..........................................

MEMENTO

McCarty pottery
Merigold
*mccartyspottery.com*

RESTAURANT

Taylor Grocery
Taylor
*taylorgrocery.com*

.............................................

SCENIC DRIVE

Natchez Trace Pkwy
*Tupelo to Natchez*

## NORTH CAROLINA

**EST. 1789 MOTTO:** *To be, rather than to be seen*

........................................................

- ⊕ STATE BIRD
  NORTHERN CARDINAL

- ✳ STATE FLOWER
  DOGWOOD

- ◈ STATE GEM
  EMERALD

- ♬ STATE SONG
  "THE OLD NORTH STATE"

---

SMALL FESTIVAL
Easterns Surf Contest
Nags Head
*surfesa.org*

........................................................

RESTAURANT
Kindred
Davidson
*kindreddavidson.com*

........................................................

BAR
The Crunkleton
Chapel Hill
*thecrunkleton.com*

........................................................

SCENIC DRIVE
Waterfall Byway, US 64
*Rosman to Murphy*

........................................................

DETOUR
Whirligig Park & Museum
Wilson
*wilsonwhirligigpark.org*

........................................................

MEMENTO
Cane Rocker
Troutman
*troutmanchairs.com*

## SOUTH CAROLINA

**EST. 1788 MOTTO:** *While I breathe, I hope*

........................................................

- ⊕ STATE BIRD
  CAROLINA WREN

- ✳ STATE FLOWER
  YELLOW JESSAMINE

- ◈ STATE GEM
  AMETHYST

- ♬ STATE SONG
  "CAROLINA"

---

SMALL FESTIVAL
Governor's Cup
Billfishing Tournament
Georgetown

........................................................

RESTAURANT
FIG
Charleston
*eatatfig.com*

........................................................

BAR
The Esso Club
Clemson
*theessoclub.com*

........................................................

SCENIC DRIVE
Maybank Hwy 700
*James Island to Rockville*

........................................................

DETOUR
Aiken Horse Track
Aiken
*aikentrainingtrack.com*

........................................................

MEMENTO
Cufflinks
Ben Silver Charleston
*bensilver.com*

# TENNESSEE

**EST.** 1796 **MOTTO:** *Agriculture and commerce*

........................................

⊕ STATE BIRD
MOCKINGBIRD

✾ STATE FLOWER
PASSION FLOWER

◈ STATE GEM
TENNESSEE RIVER PEARL

♫ STATE SONG
"TENNESSEE WALTZ"

SMALL FESTIVAL
National Storytelling
Festival
Jonesborough
*storytellingcenter.net*

........................................

RESTAURANT
Husk
Nashville
*husknashville.com*

........................................

BAR
Earnestine & Hazel's
Memphis

........................................

SCENIC DRIVE
Hwy 315
*Benton to Tellico*

........................................

DETOUR
Bluegrass Underground
Pelham
*thecaverns.com*

........................................

MEMENTO
Benton's Country Ham
Madisonville
*shop.bentonscountryham.com*

# VIRGINIA

**EST.** 1788 **MOTTO:** *Thus always to tyrants*

........................................

⊕ STATE BIRD
NORTHERN CARDINAL

✾ STATE FLOWER
AMERICAN DOGWOOD

◈ STATE ROCK
NELSONITE

♫ STATE SONG
"SWEET VIRGINIA BREEZE"

SMALL FESTIVAL
Old Fiddlers' Convention
Galax
*oldfiddlersconvention.com*

........................................

RESTAURANT
Heritage
Richmond
*heritagerva.com*

........................................

BAR
Alley Light
Charlottesville
*alleylight.com*

........................................

SCENIC DRIVE
Skyline Drive, Shenandoah NP
*Waynesboro to Front Royal*

........................................

DETOUR
Monticello
Charlottesville
*monticello.org*

........................................

MEMENTO
Heirloom Seeds
Southern Exposure Seed Exchange
*southernexposure.com*

# CITIES
# & TOWNS

Ten communities large and
small that capture the hometown
spirit of the South

# CHARLOTTESVILLE, VA

POPULATION **46,597**

SIZE **10.3 SQ MILES**

ELEVATION **594 FT**

SUNSHINE **219 DAYS**

NOTED RESIDENTS:
*Meriwether Lewis, Dave Matthews, Tina Fey*

COFFEE:
*Grit Coffee, Mudhouse, Shenandoah Joe*

This Virginia college town in Shenandoah country, home of pastoral back roads and academic verve, was undeniably shook by the vile white supremacist rallies in 2017. Thoughtful locals are approaching reflection and renewal with honesty. Two exemplars: THE JEFFERSON SCHOOL, an African-American cultural center and oral history hub, and NEW CITY ARTS, a dynamic community of artists. The city is always learning. And no visit to Charlottesville is complete without roaming UVA's campus. Snag a copy of Breece D'J Pancake's short stories at NEW DOMINION BOOKSHOP, then toss a blanket on the Rotunda lawn and enjoy Jefferson's vision of higher learning. Head west to Crozet and rub shoulders with vintners at KING FAMILY VINEYARDS; the 2014 Meritage won a recent Governor's Cup. One tried-and-true favorite dinner spot is C&O, opened in 1976 with farm-to-table ideals before the term existed. Sitting across from the old railyard [hence the name], the restaurant's century-old brick pairs well with a refined kitchen. Residents dig the cozy cocktail den ALLEY LIGHT for a nightcap, though the indie spirit at THE GARAGE, a stand-alone car-cubby turned tiny [like really tiny] venue, would make Dave Matthews proud. Bed down at the handsome TOWNSMAN, a self-described "unhotel" with rooms named after famous locals. That push-pull of tradition: Charlottesville wears it well.

---

LOCAL TO KNOW

*"The cafe is less than a ten-minute walk from where I grew up in Vinegar Hill. Since we opened in 1982, I've always been first one in, last one to leave. Fifteen-hour days. I greet everyone when they come in the door. We're the kind of place that knows your first name."*
— MEL WALKER, owner of Mel's Cafe

# LAFAYETTE, LA

POPULATION **129,626**

SIZE **53.91 SQ MILES**

ELEVATION **36 FT**

SUNSHINE **215 DAYS**

NOTED RESIDENTS:
*Earnest Gaines, George Rodrigue, Ali Landry*

COFFEE:
*Rêve, Black Cafe*

---

Recently named the "Happiest Place in America" by Harvard economists, Lafayette—the unofficial capital of Acadiana—is the perfect hub for exploring Louisiana's rich Cajun and Creole cultures. For breakfast, belly up to the counter at JOHNSON'S BOUCANIÈRE—French for smokehouse—and you're likely to hear old-timers chatter in the local Cajun dialect while you wait for a boudin-, brisket- or pulled-pork-filled biscuit. Make sure to grab a sack of fried and spiced pork cracklins alongside a few links of boudin, the locally ubiquitous rice-and-pork sausage, for the road. To sample the best of Creole cooking, head to LAURA'S II—there is no Laura's I—where softball-size scoops of rice and gravy buttress daily stewed specials, crawfish étouffée, filigree-fried pork chops and spicy, stuffed turkey wings. At the MAISON MADELEINE BED & BREAKFAST, about ten miles outside town, wake to the morning sun shimmering through Spanish moss-curtained cypress trees along LAKE MARTIN, a paddle-worthy nature preserve teeming with migratory water birds, native flora and the occasional gator. Local and traveling bands love playing the BLUE MOON SALOON & GUESTHOUSE, where ice-cold beer fuels a dance floor swarming with Cajun waltzers and fleet-footed zydeco high-steppers.

---

LOCAL TO KNOW

*"Our king cake recipe goes back more than 120 years. Each one is rolled, proofed, filled and decorated in purple for justice, gold for power and green for faith. But growing up, if you were a Keller and could count to 12, your job was bagging butter rolls by the dozen."*
— ASHLEY KELLER, Keller's Bakery Downtown

# SAVANNAH, GA

POPULATION **146,763**

SIZE **108.7 SQ MILES**

ELEVATION **49 FT**

SUNSHINE **216 DAYS**

NOTED RESIDENTS:
*Johnny Mercer, The Lady Chablis,*
*Big Boi, Juliette Gordon Lowe*

COFFEE:
*The Coffee Fox, Sentient Bean*

Meticulously laid out in 1733 by John Oglethorpe, Georgia's oldest city is also its loveliest. Savannah's mannered, moss-draped mystique radiates from the well-preserved antebellum homes and generations-old churches that stand sentry in its historic core. Start at the riverside City Hall and head south down Bull Street to walk through five of the remaining 22 squares before winding up in 30-acre FORSYTH PARK to admire its 1858 fountain [and ponder its soon-to-be-politically-corrected Confederate monument]. From there it's an easy amble over to THE GASTONIAN, a graceful B&B in adjoining 1868 mansions with 17 un-identical guest rooms; breakfast is included, but save room for BACK IN THE DAY BAKERY's biscuits. Once sated, make your way through three eras of art, architecture and history at the TELFAIR MUSEUMS, a trio of distinctive buildings that link Savannah's old-money philanthropy with its burgeoning creative class. That downtown-revitalizing force can be traced to the 1978 opening of the SAVANNAH COLLEGE OF ART AND DESIGN, best experienced via its own museum and retail shop. Similarly scene-altering has been THE GREY, where "port city Southern" fare is served in an overhauled Greyhound station. No reservations? Just slip into a booth in its diner-style bar.

---

### LOCAL TO KNOW

*"Savannah is 50 years behind, but in many ways that's a good thing. Living here, you take for granted how beautiful the squares are, how walkable the city is—even if the humidity can kill you. It's a strange, quirky place, and if you're looking for that slow-paced life, it's still here."*
— PAULA DANYLUK, owner of the Paris Market and Brocante

# THE OUTER BANKS, NC

POPULATION **28,018**

SIZE **531.98 SQ MILES**

ELEVATION **7 FT**

SUNSHINE **200 DAYS**

NOTED RESIDENTS:
*Andy Griffith, Matthew Quick*

COFFEE:
*Front Porch Cafe, Treehouse Coffee*

---

For 200 miles this narrow band of barrier islands traces the coast like a weathered picket fence. Drive the two-lane Outer Banks National Scenic Byway north until you reach tiny Duck, named for its avian visitors. Stay at the lush SANDERLING RESORT, and after morning coffee at DUCK'S COTTAGE, a 1921 hunting cottage transformed into a bookstore, head south to JOCKEY'S RIDGE, the highest living sand dune on the East Coast, where atop 6,000 dump trucks' worth of sand you can catch the sun's first rays. Next, depart for PEA ISLAND NATIONAL WILDLIFE REFUGE, a pristine 13-mile stretch of the Cape Hatteras National Seashore [where you drive your car directly onto the sand]. Climb the historic HATTERAS LIGHTHOUSE before taking a ferry to Ocracoke Island, home of the Lost Colony. History beckons in Beaufort, established in 1709, where the Old Burying Ground is home to both a revolutionary British soldier interred standing up and a girl buried inside a rum keg. Stroll along Front Street, admiring the wild horses on Shackleford Banks, just a few hundred yards away. Dine on the daily catch at the BEAUFORT GROCERY and follow it with a drink at THE BACKSTREET PUB, a watering hole so dark it feels as if former resident Blackbeard might walk in at any moment.

---

LOCAL TO KNOW

*"We have a tight-knit surf community, lifelong friends. The best time is fall, when hurricanes off the coast make swells. The shallow, sand-bottom waves produce quality barrels and good-quality rides. There's miles of peaks and waves, and you never have to surf in a crowd."*

— BOB HOVEY, co-owner of Duck Village Outfitters

# FAYETTEVILLE, AR

POPULATION **83,826**

SIZE **55.41 SQ MILES**

ELEVATION **1,400 FT**

SUNSHINE **217 DAYS**

NOTED RESIDENTS:
*Ellen Gilchrist, Edward Durell Stone, Ronnie Hawkins*

COFFEE:
*Onyx, Arsaga's*

Smell the mountain air in Fayetteville, a serene college town—the University of Arkansas Razorbacks call it home—and the perfect launch pad for exploring the art-abundant towns scattered throughout the Ozark foothills. In Fayetteville, the city streets are alive with color, part and parcel of a local PUBLIC ART INITIATIVE. Murals animate brick walls, sculptures awaken public parks and sidewalks, utility boxes buzz with paintings of insects and even storm drains pop with bright designs. An hour's drive northeast in Eureka Springs, burrowed within a dense forest, the wood-and-glass-constructed THORNCROWN CHAPEL dazzles with sunlight and inspiration. And in nearby Bentonville, the Moshe Safdie-designed CRYSTAL BRIDGES MUSEUM OF AMERICAN ART has quickly become, thanks to a Walmart heir's riches, one of the nation's premier destinations for early American and contemporary paintings. Included are works by Homer, Pollock, O'Keeffe and Rothko and an entire Frank Lloyd Wright house that once resided in New Jersey. To snag a meal any time of day, glide into THE HIVE, located in the local outpost of the always stellar 21c Museum Hotels, for a modern reimagining of country cooking, like hearty cider-braised pork shoulder with locally grown rice grits.

---

### LOCAL TO KNOW

*"Something magical happens in the wild of spring here. Deciduous trees are abundant. The air becomes fragrant with honeysuckle. Crumbling old facades are taken over with green. Nestled in these well-worn hills of the Ozarks is a distinct charm I've never seen anywhere else."*
— KATY HENRIKSEN, public radio host at KUAF

# MEMPHIS, TN

| | |
|---|---|
| POPULATION **652,717** | NOTED RESIDENTS: |
| SIZE **324 SQ MILES** | *Al Green, Kathy Bates, Shelby Foote* |
| ELEVATION **337 FT** | COFFEE: |
| SUNSHINE **218 DAYS** | *City & State, Otherlands, Muddy's* |

Memphis is musky, cool, fermented with all that's complex about the South. It is more than mallard ducks on parade and the shag-and-gilt tomb of the King. And proud Memphians don't shy from the grit-grind of the true city, past and present, honoring heroic figures like Ida B. Wells and celebrating the city's mixtape of Alex Chilton, Carla Thomas, 8Ball & MJG. Living up to the Egyptian mystery of its name, Memphis in many ways is a city of reincarnation. Wafts of smoke cover barbecue joints of world renown, circled on a million maps: Payne's, A&R, Cozy Corner and RENDEZVOUS, whose bow-tied gentlemen carry on circa-1948 dry-rubbed traditions. In Midtown, visit the MEMPHIS BROOKS MUSEUM OF ART, notably for its robust photo collection of two local sons: civil rights documentarian Ernest Withers and Willam Eggleston, godfather of color photography. For deeper historic cuts, head to the well-done STAX MUSEUM, where artists like Otis Redding and Booker T. & the M.G.'s rained hot buttered soul upon the world. And there's never a bad night to end up at EARNESTINE & HAZEL'S, a red-tinted bar with a haunted jukebox and a midnight burger worth grease drippings on your suit. Look around: This is the real-deal Memphis.

LOCAL TO KNOW

*"For 30 years Shangri-La Records has been at the intersection of Memphis music, past and present. Sun, Stax and Hi eras, yes, but also what's current in the Bluff City. The employees who've worked here read like a who's who of the music scene."*
— JARED MCSTAY & JOHN MILLER, co-owners of Shangri-La Records

# LOUISVILLE, KY

POPULATION **767,355**

SIZE **397.68 SQ MILES**

ELEVATION **466 FT**

SUNSHINE **197 DAYS**

NOTED RESIDENTS:
*Muhammad Ali, Jim James,
Jennifer Lawrence*

COFFEE:
*Highland, La Grange*

Honor Louisville's finest son, not to mention the greatest of all time, with a pilgrimage to the MUHAMMAD ALI CENTER, a museum that endeavors to shake up the world by promoting peace and justice. Walk along the city's revitalized downtown Ohio River corridor, dropping into the ANGEL'S ENVY DISTILLERY, a freethinking brand known for its port barrel- and rum cask-finished whiskeys. The local chef of the millennium is Edward Lee, the Korean-American host of *The Mind of a Chef* season three. Down in the historic Old Louisville neighborhood, Lee remixes the modern South at 610 MAGNOLIA. At the river-area MILKWOOD, Lee marries Asian flavors with Southern inspirations, like bibimbap with pulled pork. Louisville is, above all else, a quintessential cocktail town. Make sure to pop into the city's renowned hotels to scope the Golden Age barrooms, reminders of the era when Americans knew Louisville as the "Gateway to the South." Opened in 1905, the Seelbach Hotel has hosted F. Scott Fitzgerald, Al Capone and the Stones. At the Brown Hotel, nosh a legendary, spirits-reviving Hot Brown sandwich. But stay at the 21C MUSEUM HOTEL, the first in the chain's cross-South collection, where the lobby, rooms and dining areas are bedecked with contemporary art and the now iconic red penguins.

---

LOCAL TO KNOW

*"Pappy was my great-grandfather. Ours is one of the last industries where family-owned businesses make it past the second generation. You get used to things taking a long time. I'm 40, and we're making whiskey today that won't be ready until I'm in my 60s."*
— PRESTON VAN WINKLE, Old Rip Van Winkle Distillery

# BIRMINGHAM, AL

POPULATION **212,237**

SIZE **149 SQ MILES**

ELEVATION **644 FT**

SUNSHINE **210 DAYS**

NOTED RESIDENTS:
*Condoleezza Rice, Fannie Flagg, Sun Ra*

COFFEE:
*Revelator, Woodlawn Cycle Café, Caveat, Church Street, O'Henry's, Urban Standard*

The renaissance of this Alabama town—previously best known for its civil rights scars—is palpable. Downtown streets are electric with the arrival of stylish new mercantile shops, such as WINSLET & RHYS, and bars like THE ATOMIC LOUNGE, where cocktail culture shimmies with midcentury-modern flair. Sleepy forgotten neighborhoods have turned off the snooze button. In Woodlawn, shop CLUB DUQUETTE for denim, palo santo bundles and local music. In Norwood, pick up hard-to-find bourbons at LENELL'S BEVERAGE BOUTIQUE, the ultra-curated brainchild of one of the city's prodigal daughters. Reclaimed urban outdoor spaces like the Rotary Trail and Railroad Park, 19 acres of glorious green, have locals filling the streets long after bank-closing time. Just adjacent, you'll find the city's new minor league baseball stadium and the NEGRO SOUTHERN LEAGUE MUSEUM, the first organization to explicitly champion the black players, such as hometown boy Willie Mays, who forever changed the game. And amid the growth, the OG influencers of the 'Ham's finer life still flourish, such as chef célèbre Frank Stitt. There is perhaps no better way to spend an afternoon than a late lunch on the patio at his CHEZ FONFON, lingering over a game of bocce and a carafe of wine.

---

LOCAL TO KNOW

*"Music has always been important in Birmingham. Artists are always encouraging one another, venues allowing local talent to grow. From the days of Hotel to St. Paul & The Broken Bones, creativity breeds creativity, and the music feeds off that vibe."*
— SCOTT "REG" REGISTER, Birmingham Mountain Radio

---

# GREENVILLE, SC

POPULATION **67,453**

SIZE **28.8 SQ MILES**

ELEVATION **966 FT**

SUNSHINE **221 DAYS**

NOTED RESIDENTS:
*Jesse Jackson, Dorothy Allison, Kevin Garnett*

COFFEE:
*Methodical, Coffee Underground*

Once known as the "Textile Capital of the World," today Greenville is a city on the move and home to an international automotive engineering industry, including BMW and Michelin. In this Main Street-on-steroids Southern city, you'll find independent boutiques, a vibrant Saturday farmers market and a minor league baseball team [whose stadium is a mini-replica of Fenway Park]. The walkable downtown streets converge on FALLS PARK, a reclaimed mill village-turned-outdoors oasis along the Reedy River. The floating suspension LIBERTY BRIDGE offers the best views of one of the world's only urban waterfalls. Head upriver to source provisions at SWAMP RABBIT, a farmer-focused grocery/cafe/butcher/ bakery that, come the long weekend, combines all these elements— hyperlocal flours, meats and cheeses—into a rotating list of baroque pies at Swamp Pizza. Go deep on Upcountry flavors at Husk, Sean Brock's mega-ode to the Southern table. At THE ANCHORAGE, Brock alum and James Beard nominee Greg McPhee goes all in on the veggies—you can't miss the massive cornucopia-themed mural outside. Just outside of town, in the Blue Ridge Mountains, the HOTEL DOMESTIQUE is an auberge-style lodge co-owned by George Hincapie, the 17-time Tour de France cyclist.

---

LOCAL TO KNOW

*"Eight years ago, we visited during the Greenville Open Studios weekend, and the community was so generous and warm. Locals rally around young artists, from the Greenville Center for Creative Arts to Teresa Roche's Art and Light Gallery in the West End. It's why we chose to make this our home."*
— SIGNE GRUSHEVENKO, artist

# CHATTANOOGA, TN

POPULATION **177,571**

SIZE **144.6 SQ MILES**

ELEVATION **676 FT**

SUNSHINE **207 DAYS**

NOTED RESIDENTS:
*Bessie Smith, Samuel L. Jackson, Bob Corker*

COFFEE:
*Velo, Mad Priest, Goodman*

A city best known for giving its name to a frothy, ubiquitous big-band tune from the 1940s, Chattanooga has recently redefined itself on its own terms. Home to the nation's first public fiber-based internet network, Chattanooga is also the first municipality in the world to crowdfund its own custom typeface—Chatype—now seen on signage citywide. THE DWELL HOTEL, a one-time Civil War fort-turned-boutique hotel where classic Southern hospitality meets Old Hollywood style, is the perfect spot to begin explorations of this old city made new. Head riverward for the panoramic vantages of the Bluff View Art District, and make sure to stop at the HUNTER MUSEUM, the region's most comprehensive collection of American art. Walk across the Tennessee River to the boho Northside neighborhood, where small businesses thrive. Bakery and gelateria MILK & HONEY has the power to revive, no matter what ails you. At CHAMPY'S, get your fried chicken—and potluck-worthy sides—with a round of forties in custom oversize koozies. For dinner, roll into MAIN STREET MEATS, a neighborhood butcher shop serving up a contemporary take on the old steak-and-whiskey joint. Before you choo-choo on home, drive up LOOKOUT MOUNTAIN, and skip the touristy Rock City and Ruby Falls for a three-mile circular hike around Point Park.

---

LOCAL TO KNOW

*"Every time we're recruiting a candidate to move here we take the company pontoon out around the downtown waterfront and through the river gorge. This is an outdoors city. I still have a punch list of over 25 waterfalls 30 minutes from here that I still need to explore."*
— CAMERON DOODY, co-founder and president of Bellhops

---

OVER 20 ENTRIES

# ALMANAC

A deep dive into the cultural
heritage of the South through news
clippings, timelines, nomenclature
and other historical hearsay

## NUISANCES OF NOTE

| | |
|---|---|
| Beaver | *Aquatic rodents with leathery tails and webbed feet, stick-and-mud lodges flood pastures and timberlands* |
| Boll Weevil | *Long-snouted beetles and cotton's ultimate nemesis ravaged MS Delta in 1909, leading to economic ruin* |
| Burmese Python | *Stealthy and reproductively prodigious "pets" with newfound appetite for mammals of the Everglades* |
| Cicada | *Emerge in 13- or 17-year cycles, earsplitting mating calls, left-behind exoskeletons crunch underfoot* |
| Chigger | *Invisible biters bedeviling barefoot children for centuries, red welts as a summer rite of passage* |
| Cockroach | *Infamously resilient, incredibly social, the three-inch-long scramblers trigger household paranoia* |
| Emerald Ash Borer | *Hatchlings of shimmery beetles burrow into trees, block nutrient flow and require quarantine* |
| Lionfish | *This creature's 18 venomous fin rays impose feverish symptoms to Atlantic divers and fishermen* |
| Nutria | *Buck-toothed, furry marsh eaters once numbered 6,000 per square mile in South Louisiana* |
| Sandfly | *Midges found near the shore with itchy bites beating out sunburn as worst beach souvenirs* |
| Stink Bug | *Shield-shaped insects release pungent odor, a favorite of pesky little brothers everywhere* |

---

### KUDZU

Kudzu isn't a vine, merely. Kudzu is the Lord's indulgent gift to Georgians whose fathers and grandfathers permitted the land to wash away. It isn't a rapid growing vine that runs over our silver-haired friend's boxwood and camellias, only. It is the final bulwark against want and malnutrition. Either we hold the hills with this miracle plant or we go into a permanent decline. — *Channing Cope, a Georgian farmer, radio personality and columnist; June* 1948

## PIGGLY WIGGLY

On September 6, 1916, Clarence Saunders opened the first
Piggly Wiggly grocery store at 79 Jefferson Avenue in Memphis,
Tennessee. Saunders' store was the first to provide checkout
stands, mark prices on every item and, in 1937, furnish customers
with shopping carts. Below, an excerpt from an advertisement in
*The Commercial Appeal* that preceded his inaugural opening.

*The Commercial Appeal*
September 3, 1916

*Piggly Wiggly . . . Ain't That a Funny Name? The fellow that got up that
name must have a screw loose somewhere. All this may be so, but the
Piggly Wiggly knows its own business best and its business will be this: To
have no store clerks gab and smirk while folks are standing around ten deep
to get waited on. Every customer will be her own clerk, so if she wants to
talk to a can of tomatoes and kill her time, all right and well—and it seems
likely this will be a mighty lonesome chat.*

## TABASCO

Edmund McIlhenny bottled his first batch of hot sauce in 1869
on Avery Island, Louisiana. Six hundred fifty-eight bottles
were sent to area grocers, who sold them for $1. As his famous
*Capsicum frutescens* peppers grew, McIlhenny used a red stick, or
*"le petit bâton rouge,"* to check his spicy specimens for perfect ripe-
ness. In 1872, he attached a warning label to the bottles.

*CAUTION.—This Sauce should always be mixed with your gravy,
vinegar, or other condiment, before using. One or two drops are enough for
a plate of soup, meat, oysters, &c., &c.*

*It is superior in flavor to, and cheaper than any similar preparation; one
bottle being equal to a dozen of the ordinary kind.*

*Clockwise, from top left: Big Jack Johnson, Blind Boy Fuller,
Dinah Washington, Bessie Smith, Percy Mayfield, Memphis Minnie*

# BLUES LEGENDS OF NOTE

| | |
|---|---|
| Otis Rush | *Pioneer of West Side style of Chicago blues, the lefty guitarist's slow, sliding sound was major influence on Eric Clapton* |
| Percy Mayfield | *Lesser-known songwriter's hits include "Hit the Road Jack," "Please Send Me Someone to Love" and "The River's Invitation"* |
| Champion Jack Dupree | *Orphaned at eight, met Louis Armstrong at Colored Waif's Home for Boys, where he taught himself the piano* |
| Robert Nighthawk | *Boxer and electric slide guitarist schooled Muddy Waters on the whinnying ways* |
| Willie Mabon | *Pianist whose laconic vocals are best captured on "I Don't Know," later covered by the Blues Brothers* |
| Reverend Gary Davis | *Blind as an infant, learned two-finger guitar style for ragtime and blues, ordained as Baptist minister at age 41* |
| Memphis Minnie | *Hit juke circuit as a youth, becoming glamorous icon of the genre; "Bumble Bee" still has sting* |
| Tampa Red | *Recorded more than 300 jump blues tunes, led Chicago Five session band* |
| Dinah Washington | *Nimble vocalist and "Queen of the Jukebox" won over multiple genres and married seven times in her too-short life* |
| Herman "Junior" Parker | *Chitlin' Circuit big ticket and one of the first Sun Records artists, where Elvis covered his "Mystery Train"* |
| Blind Boy Fuller | *Popular Piedmont blues artist specialized in double entendre hokum songs, coined phrase "Keep on truckin'"* |
| Big Jack Johnson | *Nicknamed "Oil Man" from day job for Shell, known for edgy electric guitar, as well as acoustic mandolin prowess* |

# SIT-INS

*On February 1, 1960, four North Carolina A&T students sat down at Woolworth's "white's only" lunch counter in Greensboro, where they were refused service. The student-led nonviolent movement garnered national attention, spreading to lunch counters from Baltimore to Miami and as far west as Texas. On July 25, 1960, three black employees ate a meal at the Greensboro Woolworth counter, terminating the store's segregation policy.*

*Greensboro Record* — February 2, 1960
Marvin Sykes, "Woolworth Made Target For Demonstration Here"

A group of 20 Negro students from A&T College occupied luncheon counter seats, without being served, at the downtown F.W. Woolworth Co. Store late this morning—starting what they declared would be a growing movement. The group declared double that number will take place at the counters tomorrow. Employees of Woolworth did not serve the group and they sat from 10:30 a.m. until after noon. White customers continued to sit and get service.

*The Nashville Tennessean* — February 14, 1960
James Talley, "Lunch Counter Strikes Hit City:
100 students Appear at 3 Variety Stores; Demonstration Quiet"

An estimated 100 students—about 90 of them Negros—went on a two-hour sit-down strike at lunch counters in three Nashville variety stores yesterday after waitresses refused to serve them. It was apparently part of a nationwide passive resistance movement by Negros against lunch counter segregation.

*Richmond Times-Dispatch* — February 21, 1960
Tom Howard, "Sit-Downs At Counters Begin Here"

Six Richmond stores closed their lunch counters yesterday after a day-long series of sit-down demonstrations by about 200 Negro college students. The daytime demonstration began shortly after 9 a.m. and continued through the day. The demonstrators, nearly all students at Virginia Union University, were quiet and orderly. They while away the hours sitting at the closed counters by reading, studying textbooks they brought and talking among themselves.

# FLANNERY O'CONNOR

*Holiday* magazine
September 1961

———

Some people are genuinely affected by the sight of a peacock, even with his tail lowered, but do not care to admit it; others appear to be incensed by it. Perhaps they have the suspicion that the bird has formed some unfavorable opinion of them. The peacock himself is a careful and dignified investigator. Visitors to our place, instead of being barked at by dogs rushing from under the porch, are squalled at by peacocks whose blue necks and crested heads pop up from behind tufts of grass, peer out of bushes and crane downward from the roof of the house, where the bird has flown, perhaps for the view. One of mine stepped from under the shrubbery one day and came forward to inspect a carful of people who had driven up to buy a calf. An old man and five or six white-haired, barefooted children were piling out the back of the automobile as the bird approached. Catching sight of him, the children stopped in their tracks and stared, plainly hacked to find this superior figure blocking their path. There was silence as the bird regarded them, his head drawn back at its most majestic angle, his folded train glittering behind him in the sunlight.

*"Whut is thet thang?"* one of the small boys asked finally in a sullen voice.

The old man had got out of the car and was gazing at the peacock with an astounded look of recognition. *"I ain't seen one of them since my granddaddy's day,"* he said, respectfully removing his hat. *"Folks used to have 'em, but they don't no more."*

*"Whut is it?"* the child asked again in the same tone he had used before.

*"Churren,"* the old man said, *"that's the king of the birds!"*

The children received this information in silence. After a minute they climbed back into the car and continued from there to stare at the peacock, their expressions annoyed, as if they disliked catching the old man in the truth.

# KENTUCKY DERBY

*In 1955, Sports Illustrated sent the son of a livery stableman to cover the 81st running of the Derby. Here, an excerpt from "Kentucky: May: Saturday," by William Faulkner.*

Even before we reach the track we can hear horses—the light hard rapid thud of hooves mounting into crescendo and already fading rapidly on. And now in the gray early light we can see them, in couples and groups at canter or hand-gallop under the exercise boys. Then one alone, at once furious and solitary, going full out, breezed, the rider hunched forward, excrescent and precarious, not of the horse but simply [for the instant] with it, in the conventional posture of speed—and who knows, perhaps the two of them, man and horse both: the animal dreaming, hoping that for that moment at least it looked like Whirlaway or Citation, the boy for that moment at least that he was indistinguishable from Arcaro or Earl Sande, perhaps feeling already across his knees the scented sweep of the victorious garland.

And we ourselves are on the track now … a hundred of us now and more still coming, all craning to look in one direction into the mouth of the chute. Then it is as if the gray, overcast, slightly moist post-dawn air itself had spoken above our heads. This time the exercise boy is a Negro, moving his mount at no schooled or calculated gait at all, just moving it rapidly, getting it off the track and out of the way, speaking not to us but to all circumambience: man and beast either within hearing: "Y'awl can git out of the way too now; here's the big horse coming."

## RECORD TIMES

| TIME | WINNER | JOCKEY | YEAR |
|---|---|---|---|
| 1:59.40 | Secretariat | Ron Turcotte | 1973 |
| 1:59.97 | Monarchos | Jorge Chavez | 2001 |
| 2:00.00 | Northern Dancer | William Hartack | 1964 |
| 2:00.20 | Spend a Buck | Angel Cordero Jr. | 1985 |
| 2:00.40 | Decidedly | William Hartack | 1962 |
| 2:00.60 | Proud Clarion | Robert Ussery | 1967 |
| 2:01.00 | Grindstone | Jerry Bailey | 1996 |
| 2:01.00 | Fusaichi Pegasus | Kent Desormeaux | 2001 |

# RECORDING STUDIOS

FAME STUDIOS Muscle Shoals, AL — Aretha Franklin, *"I Never Loved a Man"*; Wilson Pickett, *"Mustang Sally"*

MUSCLE SHOALS SOUND STUDIO Sheffield, AL — The Rolling Stones, *"Brown Sugar"*; The Staple Singers, *"I'll Take You There"*

PATCHWERK RECORDING STUDIOS Atlanta, GA — OutKast, *"Ms. Jackson"*; Usher, *"You Make Me Wanna . . ."*

J&M RECORDING STUDIOS New Orleans, LA — Little Richard, *"Tutti Frutti"*; Professor Longhair, *"Tipitina"*

SUN STUDIO Memphis, TN — Johnny Cash, *"I Walk the Line"*; U2, *"Angel of Harlem"*

STAX RECORDS Memphis, TN — Otis Redding, *"Try A Little Tenderness"*; Booker T. & the M.G.s, *"Green Onions"*

RCA STUDIO B Nashville, TN — Dolly Parton, *"Jolene"*; Roy Orbison, *"Crying"*

---

## THE WRIGHT BROTHERS

"Flying Machine Soars 3 Miles in Teeth of High Wind Over
Sand Hills and Waves at Kitty Hawk on Carolina Coast"
*Virginian-Pilot*
December 18, 1903

Wilber [*sic*] Wright, the chief inventor of the machine, sat in the operator's car and when all was ready his brother unfastened the catch which held the invention at the top of the slope. . . . The little crowd of fisher folk and coast guards, who have been watching the construction of the machine with unconcealed curiosity since September 1, were amazed. They endeavored to race over the sand and keep up with the thing of the air, but it soon distanced them and continued its flight alone, save the man in the car. Steadily it pursued its way first tacking to port, then to starboard and then driving straight ahead. "It is a success," declared Orville Wright to the crowd on the beach after the first mile had been covered.

# LITERARY REVIEWS

ABSALOM, ABSALOM!
*William Faulkner*

The characters have no magnitude and no meaning because they have no more reality than a mince-pie nightmare.

*The New Yorker,* 1936

..............................

THEIR EYES WERE
WATCHING GOD
*Zora Neale Hurston*

The town of Eatonville is as real in these pages as Jacksonville is in the pages of Rand McNally; and the lives of its people are rich, racy, and authentic.

*The Saturday Review of Literature,* 1937

..............................

GERONIMO REX
*Barry Hannah*

Hannah is one of those young writers who is brilliantly drunk with words and could at gunpoint write a life story of telephone pole.

*The New York Times,* 1972

..............................

THE HEART IS A LONELY HUNTER
*Carson McCullers*

The most impressive aspect ... is the astonishing humanity that enables a white writer, for the first time in Southern fiction, to handle Negro characters with as much ease and justice as those of her own race.

*The New Republic,* 1940

..............................

LET US NOW PRAISE FAMOUS MEN
*James Agee and Walker Evans*

Mr. Evans says as much about tenant farmers in the Cotton South in his several dozen pictures as Mr. Agee says in 150,000 words of text.

*The New York Times,* 1941

..............................

THE OPTIMIST'S DAUGHTER
*Eudora Welty*

Miss Eudora has written a small novel as delicate as a piece of lace that abounds in... vocal rhythms of country folk and persons in the big, mansions, of feelings.

*St. Louis Post-Dispatch,* 1972

..............................

ALL THE KING'S MEN
*Robert Penn Warren*

It isn't a great novel or a completely finished work of art. It is as bumpy and uneven as a corduroy road ... Nevertheless, [it] is magnificently vital reading, a book so charged with dramatic tension it almost crackles with blue sparks.

*The New York Times,* 1946

# HERSCHEL WALKER

*"There's A Big Rush On To Woo Herschel Walker"*
*The Atlanta Constitution*
December 6, 1979

WRIGHTSVILLE—An icy wind had swept down from the north the night before, and in late afternoon it was still howling, kicking dust into eyes, numbing fingertips and generally making football practice torture for the Trojans of Johnson County High. In the not-so-distant past, no one outside the players would have bothered to show up—and even they might have had second thoughts. But that was before Herschel Walker.

Now, nothing so insignificant as the season's first Arctic blow could keep a fair portion of the population of Johnson County away from Trojan practices. On a typical day last week, the faithful arrived in cars from town and in pickups from out in the country, and one by one, they drifted over to where the big-time college recruiter stood, watching Herschel Walker's every nuance.

"He's really something, ain't he?" opened a leathery man in overalls.

"He certainly is," replied the recruiter, Oklahoma's Lucious Selmon.

"Y'all got a chance to get him?"

"I don't know," said Selmon. "There's a lot of competition, I know."

"Yeah, and there oughta be," said the man in overalls, with unmistakable pride. "He's the biggest thing ever happened around here." And a dozen or so others standing nearby nodded gravely in agreement. … Walker is a 6-foot-2-inch, 216-pound wonder. In street clothes, he resembles an inverted pyramid of sinew and muscle. He is defending state track champion in the 100- and 220-yard run and in the shot put. A conscientious student, he maintains a 90-plus average and is president of the school Beta Club.

And in football he is every coach's dream. As a tailback, he has gained 2,848 yards and scored 41 touchdowns this season along. "The good Lord just dropped him in here," said [Johnson County coach Gary] Phillips.

# TABBY RUINS

*The preferred building material of early colonists along the coastal southeast, tabby was an upcycled mix of quicklime, sand, water and crushed shells. It fell out of use by the 1930s, but some remnants, as layered as a mille-feuille, remain.*

### COLONIAL DORCHESTER STATE HISTORIC SITE
*Summerville, SC* — 1760s fort built by Congregationalists from Massachusetts to stave off French attacks that never came.

### CHAPEL OF EASE
*St. Helena Island, SC* — Satellite house of worship built [c. 1740] for planters who lived too far from Beaufort's St. Helena Parish.

### WORMSLOE STATE HISTORIC SITE
*Savannah, GA* — English loyalist Noble Jones' imposing house with double-hearth chimney and surrounding eight-foot walls [c. 1740].

### FORT FREDERICA NATIONAL MONUMENT
*St. Simons Island, GA* — Ghost town of Savannah founder James Edward Oglethorpe's master-planned Utopia [1736-1749] for tradesmen and "worthy poor."

### McINTOSH SUGAR MILL PARK
*St. Mary's, GA* — Former sugar cane plantation dates to 1825, thought to have first horizontal cattle-powered sugar mill.

### KINGSLEY PLANTATION
*Jacksonville, FL* — Semicircle of 25 remaining cabins built for and by slaves on Fort George Island in 1820s with shells discarded by Timucua Indians.

# HOG HAMMOCK

The lone town on Georgia's primeval Sapelo Island, Hog Hammock has fewer than 50 residents, descendants of enslaved West Africans brought here in the late 1700s to work fields of sugar cane, rice and cotton. For generations, the Gullah-Geechee culture, cultivated across the Sea Islands and marked by its sing-song Creole language, was preserved by its isolation. But that same remoteness has led to ever-dwindling communities. In Hog Hammock, reached only by boat and open only to those who've prearranged a tour, this singular heritage holds on. *sapeloislandga.org*

# EMANCIPATION

*In the decades following the Civil War, many
former slaves used newspaper want ads as a method of
finding long-lost family and friends.*

*Southwestern Christian Advocate* — New Orleans, LA
May 10, 1883

I want to find my people. I left them about fifty years ago in Smith county, Tenn. My mother's name was Lucinda Sanders; father was Major Sanders. I had two sisters, Susan and Margaret. I had two uncles, John and Harry; two aunts, Bettie and Lillie. We belonged to Squire Alexander. We lived near Carthage, Tenn. Address Maria Ross, Yazoo City, Miss., care of M. E. Church.

*The Christian Recorder* — Philadelphia, PA
1886

Information wanted of my son, Allen Jones. He left me before the war, in Mississippi. He wrote me a letter in 1853 in which he said that he was sold to the highest bidder, a gentleman in Charleston, S.C. Nancy Jones, his mother, would like to know the whereabouts of the above named person. Any information may be sent to Rev. J.W. Turner, pastor of A.M.E. Church, Ottawa, Kansas.

*The Western Appeal* — Minnesota
August 3, 1889

Martha Cobble, of Owensboro, Ky., a Colored woman formerly a slave, has searched forty years for her two sons who were sold to a New Orleans trader when they were eight and ten years of age. Recently she learned the whereabouts of both and was made happy by a visit from one of them.

*The Freeman* — Indianapolis, IN
June 22, 1895

I want to find George Hutchinson, owned in slavery days by John C. Moore. He joined the standing army in Memphis, Tenn. He was a Baptist preacher. Address Emma Cloud, Frankfort, Marshall Co., Kansas.

## TUSKEGEE UNIVERSITY

1880 ....... Alabama senator proposes deal to secure the black vote in exchange for African-American school, wins re-election

1881 ....... Governor establishes the Tuskegee Normal School for teachers; 25-year-old Booker T. Washington teaches first class

1893 ........ Architect Robert R. Taylor oversees new Science Hall, constructed entirely by students

1896 ....... Botanist/inventor George Washington Carver hired

1906 ....... Carver launches "movable school" with horse-drawn Jesup Wagon

1915 ........ Washington dies at age 59; is buried near campus chapel

1927 ....... Tuskegee becomes full four-year college

1941 ....... U.S. War Department creates "Negro pursuit squadron," trained at Tuskegee

1943 ....... Carver dies; buried across from Washington; life savings [about $60,000] bequeathed to continue agricultural research

1944 ...... Tuskegee's Dr. Frederick D. Patterson co-founds United Negro College Fund

1944 ...... School of Veterinary Medicine created [responsible for nearly 75 percent of all black vets in U.S.]

1945 ....... End of World War II, nearly 1,000 black pilots trained; the 332nd Fighter Group [Tuskegee Airmen] fly 15,000 sorties

1948 ....... Alumna Alice Coachman becomes first black woman to win Olympic gold

1953 ........ Ralph Ellison wins National Book Award for *Invisible Man*

1966 ....... Sammy Younge Jr. shot and killed in Tuskegee for using "whites-only" bathroom

1985 ....... Tuskegee attains university status, is renamed

1999 ....... Official presidential apology for infamous government-led Tuskegee Syphilis Study, begun in 1932

2007 ....... Tuskegee Airmen collectively awarded Congressional Medal of Honor

2018 ....... Dr. Lily D. McNair named first female president

## MEAT AND THREES OF NOTE

| | |
|---|---|
| Arnold's Country Kitchen | *Nashville, TN — Since 1982, a paragon steam table in a bustling red cinder block space* |
| Busy Bee Cafe | *Atlanta, GA — Deep-frying chicken since 1947 near Spelman College and Clark University* |
| Niki's West | *Birmingham, AL — Fried snapper throats, creamy corn, baby lima beans in Greek-owned cafeteria* |
| Bertha's Kitchen | *Charleston, SC — Gullah-inspired, sister-run institution with fried whiting, pigs' feet, okra soup* |
| Bully's Restaurant | *Jackson, MS — Expect red trays of yams, collards, oxtails and chitterlings at family icon* |
| Mary Mac's Tea Room | *Atlanta, GA — The city's official dining room, eat family-style and save room for cobbler* |
| Johnny's Restaurant | *Homewood, AL — Family lineage runs deep at this Greek-inflected newcomer with squash casserole and Keftedes* |
| The Little Tea Shop | *Memphis, TN — Crumble the corn sticks into steaming bowls of turnip greens, lunch only* |
| Martin's Restaurant | *Montgomery, AL — Pulley bones of chicken, pineapple-cheese casserole, potatoes swimming in gravy* |
| Martha Lou's Kitchen | *Charleston, SC — Pink-painted classic with fried pork chops, baked macaroni and giblet rice* |
| The Four Way | *Memphis, TN — Corner lunch spot in Soulsville that's steeped in civil rights history of the city* |
| Mama Dip's Kitchen | *Chapel Hill, NC — Beloved founder and namesake Mildred Council passed away in 2018* |
| Weaver D's | *Athens, GA — Sweet potato soufflé and best motto in the biz: "Automatic for the People"* |
| Swett's Restaurant | *Nashville, TN — Since 1954, a happy buffet line of country fixins just a whistle from Fisk* |

# THE MASTERS

1931 ........ Bobby Jones buys 360-acre Fruitland Nurseries in Augusta for $70,000

1934 ....... Precursor to the first Masters Tournament played on Jones' private golf club, Augusta National

1935 ........ Gene Sarazen's "shot heard 'round the world" double eagle to force playoff

1943 ....... Tournament suspended, livestock raised on grounds for war effort

1948 ....... Pimiento cheese and egg salad sandwiches made by Herndon family, of Augusta

1949 ....... First green jacket awarded to Masters champion

1956 ....... CBS begins televising the tournament, covering only final four holes

1958 ....... Term "Amen Corner" [11, 12 and 13] first used in *Sports Illustrated*

1960 ....... First time Jack Nicklaus, Arnold Palmer and Gary Player compete together

1966 ....... Nicklaus first to win two consecutive Masters

1975 ....... Bunker sand replaced by now-signature quartz white feldspar for tournament

1977 ....... Longtime chairman Clifford Roberts commits suicide on banks of Ike's Pond

1980 ....... Spaniard Seve Ballesteros wins, becoming first European champion

1982 ....... Dave Loggins' soothing piano theme debuts on CBS television coverage

1983 ........ Players allowed to bring their own caddies for the first time

1986 ....... Nicklaus wins record sixth Masters

1989 ....... First year for Jim Nantz to anchor CBS coverage

1990 ....... Augusta National accepts its first black member, Ron Townsend

1996 ....... Greg Norman loses six-stroke lead on final round in epic collapse

1997 ....... Tiger Woods, only 21, wins first Masters by 12 strokes

2012 ....... Condoleezza Rice becomes first female member of Augusta National

2012 ....... Bubba Watson hooks wedge through trees to win in sudden death

2015 ....... Jordan Spieth ties Masters record of 18-under par

2017 ....... Green jacket found at thrift store auctions for $139,000

2018 ....... CBS runs only four minutes of commercials per hour of coverage

# JIMMY CARTER

"Carter Once Saw a UFO on
'Very Sober Occasion'"
*The Atlanta Constitution*
September 14, 1973

Gov. Jimmy Carter doesn't scoff at people who report UFO sightings, because he saw one himself about three years ago. And, Carter quipped, "it was on a very sober occasion."

Carter said he saw a blue, disc-shaped object during a campaign stop in Leary, a South Georgia town in the same general area where numerous UFOs have been reported recently.

The object came into view as Carter and several members of the Leary Lions Club stood outside the hall where Carter was to speak. All the members of the group observed the object for about five to ten minutes, Carter said. He immediately went to a tape recorder and dictated a description of what he remembers as "a very remarkable sight."

"It was about 30 degrees above the horizon and looked about as large as the moon. It got smaller and changed to a reddish color and then got larger again," Carter recalled.

Carter speculated that the UFO "was probably an electronic occurrence of some sort," rather than a visitation from outer space. At any rate, the governor said, "it was obviously there, and obviously unidentified."

# NATURAL WONDERS

———

CAVE
Neversink Pit, AL

WATERFALL
Fall Creek Falls, TN

SWAMP
Atchafalaya Basin, LA

SAND DUNE
Jockey's Ridge, NC

BALD
Grassy Ridge Bald, NC

SYNCHRONIZED FIREFLIES
Elkmont, TN

KARST
Devils Den, FL

WATERSLIDE
Sliding Rock, NC

PRECIOUS GEMS
Crater of Diamonds, AR

SALT DOME
Avery Island, LA

ARCH
Natural Bridge, VA

PETRIFIED FOREST
Flora, MS

CANYON
Providence Canyon
State Park, GA

MOONBOW
Cumberland Falls, KY

# FISHING AND BIG-GAME RECORDS

LARGEMOUTH BASS
George W. Perry
Montgomery Lake, GA 6/2/32
22 LBS 4 OZS

SMALLMOUTH BASS
David Hayes
Dale Hollow Lake, TN 7/9/55
11 LBS 15 OZS

BLUE CATFISH
Richard Nicholas Anderson,
Kerr Lake, VA 6/18/11
143 LBS

TURKEY
David Cody Guess
Lyon County, KY 4/21/15
37.6 LBS

ALLIGATOR GAR
Alvin Bonds
Arkansas River, AR 7/31/64
215 LBS

ALLIGATOR
Mandy Stokes
Camden, AL 8/16/14
1,011.5 LBS

TARPON
David Prevost
Grand Isle, LA 10/15/15
246 LBS 6 OZS

WHITE-TAILED DEER (NON-TYPICAL)
Mandy Stokes
Camden, AL 8/16/14
312.375, 47 POINTS

---

## ODE TO THE MINT JULEP

*J. Soule Smith*, c. 1890

Then comes the zenith of man's pleasure. Then comes the julep—the
mint julep. Who has not tasted one has lived in vain. The honey of
Hymettus brought no such solace to the soul; the nectar of the Gods
is tame beside it. It is the very dream of drinks, the vision of sweet
quaffings ... When it is made, sip it slowly. August suns are shining, the
breath of the south wind is upon you. It is fragrant, cold and sweet—it is
seductive. No maiden's kiss is tenderer or more refreshing, no maiden's
touch could be more passionate. Sip it and dream—it is a dream itself.
No other land can give you so much sweet solace for your cares; no other
liquor soothes you in melancholy days. Sip it and say there is no solace
for the soul, no tonic for the body like old Bourbon whiskey.

*In New Orleans, Chris McMillian, bartender at Revel Cafe & Bar,
will offer a recitation of Smith's poetry while crafting the cocktail.*

## STARS FELL ON ALABAMA

*Carl Cramer, 1934*

Alabama felt a magic descending, spreading, long ago. Since then it
has been a land with a spell on it—not a good spell, always. Moons, red
with the dust of barren hills, thin pine trunks barring horizons, fester-
ing swamps, restless yellow rivers, are all part of a feeling—a strange
certainty that above and around them hovers enchantment—an emana-
tion of malevolence that threatens to destroy men through dark ways of
its own. It is difficult to translate this feeling into words, yet almost every
visitor to this land has known it and felt in some degree what I felt with
increasing wonder during the six years I lived there. The stranger is more
apt to realize that sorcery is at work on these people and know that the
land on which they live is its apprentice. What the strange influence is
or when it began is a matter for debate. It is a legend that the great chief
Tush-ka-lusa, upon the accidental death of his son at the hands of one of
De Soto's men, drew himself up to his seven-foot height and, standing
over his dead boy's body, called down upon all white invaders of this land
the vengeance of the Great Spirit. And it is pointed out as one of many
proofs of the power of his curse that from that day to this no year has
passed in which the Black Warrior River [named for the giant redskin] has
not claimed at least one victim. Others say that the enchantment began
in the year that two squaws in a Cherokee tribe, whose tepees were pitched
near what is now the town of Oxford, Alabama, bore on the same day
sons that were spotted as the leopard. The mothers were tried for witch-
craft and sentence to be burned—but when the flames licked about their
bound feet the earth yawned and took them and all the tribe into itself.
They lie now beneath the bottomless pit that is filled by the clear waters of
Blue Pond. So the witch-mothers triumphed and they still rule Alabama.
But those who really know, the black conjure women in their weathered
cabins along the Tombigbee, tell a different story. They say that on the
memories of the oldest slaves their fathers knew there was one indelible
imprint of an awful event—a shower of stars over Alabama. Many an Ala-
bamian to this day reckons dates from "the year the stars fell"—though
he and his neighbor frequently disagree as to what year of our Lord may
be so designated. All are sure, however, that once upon a time stars fell on
Alabama, changing the land's destiny. What has been written in eternal
symbols was thus erased—and the region has existed ever since, unreal
and fated, bound by a horoscope such as controls no other country.

# ROAD TRIPS

Soulful experiences that take
travelers into the heart of the
American South

# THE SOUTHERN EPIC
## 14-DAY

Wrought with lush landscapes and brutal histories, any true journey explores the complexities of the South: a beautiful, crooked road of misty mountains and barrier islands and sleepy small towns, collectively possessing a strange and utopian pull on the American imagination. And across time, place and narrative, over crickets and katydids, what remains is a kind of golden song, the meeting of African and Celt, lonesome notes and glory reprise.

———

1.WASHINGTON, D.C. 2.VIRGINIA WINE COUNTRY
3.AYDEN 4.RALEIGH-DURHAM
5.WESTERN CAROLINA AND THE SMOKIES
6.BLACKBERRY FARM 7.NASHVILLE 8.ATLANTA
9.ALABAMA FOLK ART 10.MONTGOMERY
11.OXFORD 12.HOT SPRINGS
13.CAJUN COUNTRY 14.NEW ORLEANS

**DAY 1**

## WASHINGTON, D.C.

The long, tangled journey south begins at the National Museum of African American History and Culture.

Arguably the most eagerly anticipated museum opening in the nation's history when it launched in 2016, the NATIONAL MUSEUM OF AFRICAN AMERICAN HISTORY AND CULTURE stands apart from its Smithsonian brethren. Deemed the "Blacksonian" by cultural critic Wesley Morris, its bronze-filigreed ziggurat shape shimmers with vitality and purpose next to the Mall's staid marble everything. From the subterranean history exhibits to the top floor's art- and music-focused galleries, the museum chronicles the African-American experience from the Middle Passage to the White House. Here, a sunken slave ship finds a home alongside Nat Turner's Bible, Emmett Till's glass-topped casket and Parliament-Funkadelic's aluminum-plated Mothership.

> "The museum's **SWEET HOME CAFÉ** feels like a museum within a museum and reminds its audience of the scope of the African-American culinary contribution."
> —Tom Sietsema, *Washington Post* food critic

**DAY 2**

## VIRGINIA WINE COUNTRY

With a viticulture stretching back to 1609, Virginia is for wine lovers.

CHRYSALIS VINEYARDS, MIDDLEBURG

Jenni McCloud champions Norton, *Vitis aestivalis*, Virginia's own native grape. Check out Todd Kliman's *The Wild Vine* for the juicy backstory.

..............................................................................

LINDEN VINEYARDS, LINDEN

Home to the state's wine-growing prophet and educator, Jim Law, a VA wine icon, circa 1983. Sip a glass of his Hardscrabble Chardonnay.

..............................................................................

RDV VINEYARDS, DELAPLANE

Perch atop this granite hillside and enjoy the Lost Mountain cab-sauv blend, among the state's most sought after wines.

## AYDEN, NC
**DAY 3**

Experience low-and-slow delights chopped with love (Carolina-style) at the Skylight Inn.

In eastern North Carolina, barbecue die-hards dictate that pitmasters go the whole hog. Literally. Here, pigs, weighing upward of 150 pounds, are slowly smoked over fresh hickory coals from dusk to dawn. No place does whole hog better than THE SKYLIGHT INN, where a replica in miniature of the nation's Capitol dome glistens from atop the dining room. Sam Jones, who runs the family restaurant today, jokes that his mom used to put hog grease in his milk bottle. "My first job at the Skylight was wiping off tables and filling the drink box. I was nine," says Jones. And the Skylight style of barbecue is notoriously simple. "Eastern North Carolina gets a bad rap for being this chopped, mushy, vinegar-soaked whatever. We take a whole animal and cook it over a bed of oak coals for 18 hours. Salt, pepper, a dash of hot sauce and apple cider vinegar. Chopped pork, coleslaw and cornbread. At Skylight, 90 percent of guests are gonna get that." And that trio, eaten together, is transcendent.

**BBQ TOUR:** Check out Grady's in Dudley, Wilber's in Goldsboro and Sam Jones' new joint in Winterville.

# RALEIGH-DURHAM, NC

This trio of high-IQ Piedmont towns is a
cultural paragon of the future South.

Young, smart and on an upward trajectory, the Triangle metro area is
humming with a cultural trifecta of food, drink and art. Revel in the
region's storytelling richness at THE MONTI, an open-mic performa-
tive showcase of personal tales. Brews at FULLSTEAM BREWERY are a
must for beers with a farm-to-glass bent: sweet potato, sorghum,
basil and any other local flavors Sean Lilly Wilson can get his hands
on. Grab a sack of baked goods at BABY SCRATCH, the newest creation
from pie queen Phoebe Lawless, before heading to Raleigh, site of the
recently expanded NORTH CAROLINA MUSEUM OF ART and its sumptu-
ous sculpture garden. If it's a Saturday, visit the CARRBORO FARMERS'
MARKET for a kaleidoscope of produce that nourishes area chefs and
home cooks alike. For dinner, reserve a table at CROOK'S CORNER in
Chapel Hill—order the region's apex shrimp and grits and cult-
favorite Atlantic Beach Pie—or head back to Raleigh for a date with
POOLE'S DINER—save room for the famous mac and cheese. Need a
late night? CAT'S CRADLE in Chapel Hill, one of the South's premier
music venues, has hosted Nirvana, R.E.M. and Public Enemy.

# WESTERN CAROLINA AND THE SMOKIES

Get outside, where lush and rambling
topographies guarantee adventure.

WATERFALL

Two trails to LINVILLE FALLS [1.4 or 1.6 miles round trip] offer spectacular
views of the northern Blue Ridge Mountains' highest-volume waterfalls.

............................................................................................

FOREST

The PINK BEDS TRAIL in Pisgah National Forest is a five-mile, nearly
level loop through a scattering of wildflowers and other wildlife.

............................................................................................

CREEK

Tennessee trout-whisperer ROB FIGHTMASTER knows every unnamed
Smoky stream and will gladly guide you into the backcountry.

| DAY | **BLACKBERRY FARM, TN** |
| --- | --- |
| **6** | Renowned worldwide for refined Southern hospitality (albeit at four-digit prices), this foothills retreat absolutely lives up to the hype. |

| TIME | ACTIVITY |
| --- | --- |
| 6 AM | Misty-morning sunrises through the low-lying veil of Smoky Mountain clouds are worth the early call time. Valentine coffee, hilltop rocking chair: morning glory. |
| 8 AM | Take breakfast at the Main House and linger over farm-fresh eggs and house-made jams from the property's gardens. |
| 10 AM | At the newly expanded Wellhouse spa, the options are near limitless, from a Muscle Melt massage to the Sorghum Beautifying Body Treatment. Stay outdoors for guided yoga and meditation sessions or a deep-forest hike. |
| 1 PM | Grab a box lunch of farm-made cheeses and charcuterie and take a drive on the back roads around Walland. |
| 4 PM | Find Jeff Ross, farmstead school manager, and take a tour of the garden rows, all full of heirloom agrarian magic. |
| 6 PM | Sip a saison from Blackberry's own brewery and imbibe in the spectacular, like when hundreds of ladybugs deem you worthy of their affection outside the white clapboard chapel. |
| 8 PM | Sup in The Barn, the cathedral-like restaurant that has quickly become one of the most enviable tables in the world. Expect haute-Appalachian cuisine and the deepest of wine and whiskey collections. |
| 12 AM | Crawl into bed, whether in your country antiques-styled room or individual Hill Cottage; as if by magic, a wood-burning fire will greet your return. |

TIP: *Though guests get first dibs on dinner reservations, it's possible, with some advance planning, to dine at the property even if you can't swing an overnight stay.*

## NASHVILLE, TN

DAY 7

Writer Drew Bratcher shares a native's memory of the most famous bluegrass joint in the world.

One Sunday night, at the STATION INN in Nashville, I watched an old man get to his feet and play the first chord of a bluegrass song. He had a gold front tooth and wore pressed blue jeans. For an hour, he had quietly fingered his guitar as pickers in folding chairs traded solo after solo and the crowd, a couple hundred flush, nodded along. Now, at a lull in the jam, he strummed and halted as if calling the house to order, then into the not quite silence he sang: *"I remember the night, little darling | We were talking of days gone by | When you told me you always would love me | That for me your love would never die."* And it was as if the lines had lit a fuse. First the inner circle of pickers, then the outer, and then what felt like the whole damn room joined in the singing. Even the ones not singing were sort of mouthing the words, and I wondered how many times the song had filled the club through the decades and about how, even as it played, hipsters and high-rises had displaced hobos and hookers on the streets outside, about how mayors and quarterbacks had come and gone, big floods and bad tornadoes too, and I thought about the future of Music City and how we could have been doing a lot worse, and possibly not much better, than singing, if not in perfect harmony, then at least in unison: *"O they tell me your love is like a flower | In the springtime blossoms so fair | In the fall they wither away dear | And they tell me that's the way of your love."* 402 12th Ave S, stationinn.com

---

## ATLANTA, GA

DAY 8

A dizzying ten-mile stretch of global cuisine serves up the expansive flavors of the New South.

Barbecue banh mi. Lengua tacos. Kimchi stew. And that's just one roadside shopping center dotting the jam-packed restaurant corridor between Buckhead and Duluth. Atlanta eaters call this taste bud paradise BUFORD HIGHWAY, a mashup of ethnic foodways that's perhaps a more bona fide picture of "Southern food" today than anywhere else in the region. Among hundreds of world-class spots, spin the globe at Pho Dai Loi #2, El Rey del Taco and Yet Tuh.

ALABAMA

Howard Finster
VALLEY HEAD

Jimmy Lee Sudduth
FAYETTE

Lonnie Holley
HARPERSVILLE

Mose Tolliver

MONTGOMERY

SEALE

Boykin

Gee's Bend Quiltmakers

Hickory Hill

BERNICE SIMS

BUTCH ANTHONY

MUSEUM OF WONDER

## ALABAMA FOLK ART

This universe of Yellowhammer artists shows the brilliant, ingenious, often spiritual nature of the beloved Southern vernacular.

When one considers the starry sky of creativity born in the South, across mediums and eras and state lines, the magic of the region's folk artists shines brightest. And no state captures the beauty and lore quite like Alabama. Outsider, primitive, even folk: The terminology typically used doesn't do the work justice. Howard Finster, Bernice Sims, Jimmy Lee Sudduth, Mose Tolliver, the Gee's Bend quilters—these visionaries explored lesser-known narratives and provocative ideas, often with rustic materials and inventive techniques. They are American masters, self-trained or not. And today, artists such as Butch Anthony and Lonnie Holley continue this rich lineage of the Southern visual patois, exhibiting the quiet genius and prophetic impulse of those otherworldly creators who came before.

*To explore the world of Alabama folk art, visit Marcia Weber Art Objects gallery in Wetumpka, Butch Anthony's Museum of Wonder in Seale and the Birmingham Museum of Art.*

---

DAY 10

## MONTGOMERY, AL

Alabama's capital, once an epicenter for racial injustice, is now forthright in its reckoning.

Standing beneath the cast-iron fountain at Court Square, gaze up the six broad blocks of Dexter Avenue to formative moments in the American story. The bus stop to your left is where Rosa Parks refused her seat to a white passenger, beginning the Montgomery Bus Boycott. And the Italianate three-story to your right is where the Confederacy telegrammed General Beauregard to fire on Fort Sumpter, thus beginning the Civil War. Martin Luther King Jr. took his first post as pastor at Dexter Baptist up the hill, and on the steps of the Capitol, George Wallace famously declared, "Segregation forever." In full view of its history, Montgomery is now home to progressive policy torchbearers like the Southern Poverty Law Center and the Equal Justice Initiative, which spurred the building of the Legacy Museum and Lynching Memorial. Only a visit captures its tectonic impact. Poignant, painful and mandatory.

<table>
<tr><td>DAY<br>11</td><td>OXFORD, MS<br>Poet Beth Ann Fennelly shares a personal memory<br>from the literary capital of the South.</td></tr>
</table>

When I go running, I often wind through St. Peter's Cemetery, past the grave of Barry Hannah, past Colonel Falkner's obelisk, over to his great-grandson's grave. I peer at the graveside offerings, flowers, flags, notes and always liquor bottles, as the tradition is to take a swig and then offer one to Mr. Bill. Certain gatherings—the Oxford Conference for the Book is one—don't seem complete without a late-night passing of brown liquor at his grave [I confess—maybe once or twice, an empty could have borne the faint imprint of my lipstick]. Once, a few years back, I found on his tombstone a clump of Mardi Gras beads and a "Happy 21st Birthday" hat. My husband [novelist Tom Franklin] and I are far from the end, we hope, so why have we bought plots in this cemetery? I want to set my weight down in a place where a youth marks the passage to adulthood with a midnight toast to William Faulkner. Oxford, Mississippi: You're home, eternally.

---

### ICONIC BOOKSELLERS
Check out SQUARE BOOKS in Oxford, LEMURIA BOOKS in
Jackson and TURNROW BOOKS in Greenwood.

## DAY 12

### HOT SPRINGS, AR

These curative waters have been rejuvenating the spirit since time immemorial.

According to local lore, warring indigenous American tribes, who called the area the "Valley of the Vapors," would practice peace while soaking in Hot Springs' restorative thermal waters, which flow like magma beneath this mountaintop town. Centuries later, national newspaper advertisements touted the city's Bathhouse Row as "America's greatest resort the year around. Where hope is renewed, disease and pain washed away and joyous health restored." Visitors followed by the thousands to soak in bathhouses like the BUCKSTAFF, still a good place to get thermal. During the Roaring '20s, the town's tranquil isolation brought gangsters looking for a hideout. Grand casinos and back-alley gambling parlors sprung up. On the lam for seven months, Lucky Luciano was finally arrested outside a bathhouse. Al Capone visited often, especially when Chicago got too "hot." The crime boss liked to rent rooms by the floor for his crew at the luxurious ARLINGTON HOTEL, where you can still be treated like a capo.

## DAY 13

### CAJUN COUNTRY, LA

Pay your respects to the inimitable French heritage of Southern Louisiana.

Growing up in the Cajun prairie town of Eunice, Marc Savoy had a singular obsession: the accordion. A squeezebox savant, by age 20 he could not only play but build accordions from scratch. In 1966, he opened the SAVOY MUSIC CENTER, an accordion workshop and gathering spot for local musicians and cultural devotees. Each Saturday morning, from 9 a.m. till noon, the Savoy Music Center hosts an acoustic jam session, where anyone is invited to participate, spectate and dance. This is Cajun music in its unadulterated state, according to Savoy: "No glitz, no Cool Whip, no glamour." Bring a box of boudin from the Best Stop Supermarket in the nearby town of Scott to share with the crowd to ensure friends for life.

> **CAJUN CLASSICS:** Whiskey River Landing, *Henderson*, Bayou Teche Brewing, *Arnaudville*, Cajun Claws, *Abbeville*

## NEW ORLEANS, LA

Eat, drink and be merry in a town that
never eighty-sixes the joie de vivre.

*For 300 years, New Orleans has ruled the region's culinary landscape. Between a coastal bounty and generations of immigrants [French, Spanish, Sicilian, Isleño and West African] all stewing their flavors together, eating big in NOLA has always been, well, easy.*

#### CHARBROILED OYSTERS: CASAMENTO'S

Flame-licked bivalves, bubbling with butter, lemon, garlic and Parmesan.
4330 *Magazine St, casamentosrestaurant.com*

#### TROUT MEUNIÈRE AMANDINE: GALATOIRE'S

Fried Louisiana trout, soaked in lemony brown butter and crowned
with sliced almonds. 209 *Bourbon St, galatoires.com*

#### MUFFULETTA: CENTRAL GROCERY

A monster of a sandwich since 1906, loaded with salumi and marinated olive salad, made popular by Sicilian immigrants-turned-green grocers. 923 *Decatur St, centralgrocery.com*

#### FRIED SHRIMP/OYSTER PO'BOY: PARKWAY BAKERY & TAVERN

The king of the working man's lunch. Made exclusively on crusty
Leidenheimer French bread. 538 *Hagan Ave, parkwaypoorboys.com*

#### TURTLE SOUP: COMMANDER'S PALACE

The rich sherry-spiked proof that everything out of the Louisiana
swamps is delicious. 1403 *Washington Ave, commanderspalace.com*

#### SATSUMA SNO-BLIZ: HANSEN'S

Velvety-smooth ice crammed high into paper bowls, doused in sweet
homemade flavors and spooned into hot summer nights. 4801
*Tchoupitoulas St, snobliz.com*

#### BARBECUE SHRIMP: PASCAL'S MANALE

No wood, no fire. Just fresh head-on Gulf shrimp swimming in
a tight pool of butter, garlic, Worcestershire and hot sauce.
1838 *Napoleon Ave, pascalsmanale.com*

#### SAZERAC: ARNAUD'S FRENCH 75 BAR

Find master bartender Chris Hannah and ask him about the 1830s apothecary who invented the sazerac. 813 *Rue Bienville, arnaudsrestaurant.com*

# THE GREAT GULF COAST
## 7-DAY

Lapping the southern edge of the region, the Gulf of Mexico is a kind of salty backwater—America's Third Coast—transforming as it's traced along two-lane highways, west to east and farther, from the chocolaty river delta that's a sportsman's paradise, to the sugar coastline between Orange Beach and Apalachicola, bending down with the mystery springs and mangroves of Florida [a state itself that's part Southern, part "maybe the South"], a place of discovery still.

---

1. VENICE  2. BILOXI & OCEAN SPRINGS
3. ORANGE BEACH  4. SANTA ROSA TO PORT ST. JOE
5. FLORIDA SPRINGS  6. SANIBEL ISLAND
7. THE KEYS

| DAY |
|:---:|
| 1 |

### VENICE, LA

Spend a day casting into one of the most
prolific fishing habitats on the planet.

We were born and raised in New Orleans, and grew up fishing this
coast our whole lives. The diversity of fish you can catch here is un-
touchable: yellowfin tuna, bull redfish, bonita, triple tail, mangrove
snapper, marlin, cobia. When you see a 40-inch redfish in two feet
of water, you'll just sight-cast and watch them come up. Something
like buck fever takes over. This last stretch of Mississippi River is a
mix of marsh and Gulf. The river dumps all its nutrients into Port
Sulfur and south, making this America's Great Barrier Reef. And for
a long time, Venice was our hidden gem. The closest grocery store is
an hour away, and forever all that was here was fishing and oil. When
the BP spill happened, millions of dollars were spent to promote the
area and bring it back. It's still way out there, a frontier, and it may
not be the fanciest place, but it's our place. —*Moe and Eric Newman,
Journey South Outfitters*

**PLAN YOUR TRIP:** *Check out the Louisiana Wildlife and Fisheries website
for detailed information on species-by-species regulations and seasons
[wlf.louisiana.gov]. For anglers looking to combine Venice and New Orleans,
note that it's only a 75-mile drive on LA-23 between the two.*

---

#### LOUISIANA GUIDES

Journey South Outfitters, Venice
*journeysouthoutfitters.com*

Calmwater Charters, Grand Isle
*calmwatercharters.net*

Fish Venice Charters, Venice
*fishvenicecharters.com*

Reel Shot Guide Service, Venice
*reelshotfishing.com*

**BILOXI & OCEAN SPRINGS, MS**

Look through the lens of its artists to see the coastal glory of the Hospitality State.

Just east of New Orleans, two museums animate a pair of Mississippi beach towns. No artist better captured the literal and abstract fluidity of Gulf Coast life than Walter Inglis Anderson. The WALTER ANDERSON MUSEUM OF ART in Ocean Springs explores the life and work of the American painter through his watercolors, linoleum block prints and writing [Anderson's older brother, Peter, was an acclaimed ceramist in his own right, having founded the nearby Shearwater Pottery in 1928, a worthy diversion when in the area]. Just across the waters of Biloxi Bay, the OHR-O'KEEFE MUSEUM OF ART houses the experimental fired-clay creations of George Ohr, nicknamed the "Mad Potter of Biloxi." The Frank Gehry-designed building is as weird and wonderful as the ceramics inside.

**ORANGE BEACH, AL**

Spend a long afternoon at this notorious (in a good way) state-line beach bar.

Sometimes you just gotta walk the line. The FLORA-BAMA, a honky-tonk oyster bar that straddles the Alabama/Florida state line at Perdido Key, is the last of the great Southern roadhouse watering holes. An Alabama bar so iconic local beach bum-turned-big shot Jimmy Buffett composed two songs about the place. If you happen to turn up during the Annual Interstate Mullet Toss, lucky you. Otherwise, suck down fresh Gulf oysters. Order a few pounds of royal red shrimp or crawfish, when in season. Stroll the powdered beaches. And go easy on the Bushwacker frozen cocktails, a potent rum-coconut-chocolate milkshake. Either way, you probably won't remember tomorrow.

> **IF THE FLORA-BAMA** sounds too rowdy, get your
> Gulf seafood fix at the Royal Oyster in Gulf Shores.

DAY
4

## SANTA ROSA TO PORT ST. JOE, FL

Fried-grouper sandwiches, sand-dollar beaches, Buffett's greatest
hits: Welcome to 100 miles of Old Florida. The 331 Bridge
spans Choctawatchee Bay and drops down near the Red Bar,
hopping, bluesy cottage with serious crab cakes. Follow 30A t

...cture-perfect cloisters—Seaside, WaterColor, Alys and Rosemary—then
...rough Panama City's 1959 Goofy Golf. In Port St. Joe, the "Forgotten
...ast" begins. It's a down-home Amalfi, a sunburnt Nantucket. Stop for
...sters at Indian Pass Raw Bar, then explore St. Joseph's Peninsula, dunes
...aying with muhly and sea oats, crystal-blue waters calling your name.

| DAY 5 |
|---|

## FLORIDA SPRINGS
Soak up and paddle down the pristine
spring waters of Central Florida.

GINNIE SPRINGS, GILCHRIST COUNTY

Cold and crystalline turquoise waters perfect for a dip, snorkel or dive;
an on-site dive shop provides tours of Ginnie's limestone caverns.

...........................................................................

THREE SISTERS SPRINGS, CRYSTAL RIVER

Snorkeling and paddling, except during the winter months,
when migratory manatees come to snowbird; the boardwalk offers
year-round access.

...........................................................................

CHASSAHOWITZKA SPRINGS, CITRUS COUNTY

Affectionally known as the Chaz, this group of a dozen springs brims with
calm, kayak-able waters; warm lagoons; and wildlife.

| DAY 6 |
|---|

## SANIBEL ISLAND, FL
The wild world's a stage on this Gulf
barrier island south of Fort Myers.

GET ON THE WATER

Put in a paddle on the Great Calusa Blueway,
a 190-mile canoe-and-kayak trail of waterways
where the lumbering sea cows like to occasionally
surprise visitors with a gentle bump.

SHELL OUT

Learn everything you never knew you wanted to
know about mollusks and their shells from mala-
cologists at the quirky Bailey-Matthews National
Shell Museum.

STAY

At the Island Inn, find lawn games, kayak and
bicycle rentals, a shell-washing station and beach-
front cottages and rooms that stretch along 550
feet of shore.

EAT

It's all about cold beer, a grouper sandwich, conch
fritters and BYOF [bring your own fish] at the
Lazy Flamingo.

**DAY 7**

## FLORIDA KEYS

Take the Overseas Highway into the land of conch
sellers and rum drinks at the literal end of the road.

It's 109 miles driving from Key Largo to the tip of Key West. Highway
1 pencils a southwesterly path, a remarkable passage, really, over these
stony martyrs and shipwreck isles. Plantation Key, Long Key, Duck
Key, Ramrod and Little Torch, Sugarloaf and Summerland. No Name
Key. As Joy Williams wrote, the Keys have a "seedy tropicality" to them.
Money made by Flagler's railroad and '80s drug smuggling, fishing
charters and snowbird vacation deals. Offshore hulls wither on cinder
blocks, orchids sellers post up at flea markets, jacaranda and bougain-
villea swamp over plank fences. Yes, the Keys certainly have moments
of splendor—The Moorings, Cheeca Lodge, Little Palm, Marquesa
Hotel. All deliver a Caribbean sophistication. And the natural island
beauty can be found combing Bahia Honda State Park with the herons,
snorkeling shipwrecks in the National Marine Sanctuary. But what's
uncanny and strange and reckless and seductive about the Keys is the
conch-republic state of mind baked into sand and reef and ramshackle
dive. Anywhere else in the South, this spine of Keys would be considered "the country," those way-out-there reaches, especially past the
Seven Mile Bridge, where seashells spell out the address, where phi-
losophers track hurricanes and where everyone, long-timers and new-
comers alike, scans the same sunset horizon every late afternoon for
the "mountains of molten gold" that stopped Audubon in his tracks.

# THE SEA ISLANDS

*South Carolina, Georgia*

AVG TEMP
**76 HIGH, 55 LOW**

SUNRISE
**6:23 AM**

SUNSET
**8:27 PM**

RAINY DAYS PER MONTH
**10**

TRIP COST
**$2250 FOR 2**

SEASONAL ACTIVITIES
**BOATING, ART WALKS, BEACHCOMBING**

Time is a slippery thing along the Sea Island coast, a marshy waterworld of oak hammocks, shrimp docks and sleepy towns, all lilted with a sing-song accent that, together, conjures up a kind of magic that's rare to find in America, if not the world. This is the Lowcountry. Her saintly capital is Charleston, with a rainbow of fine houses and a tableful of James Beard Awards. Southward from the historic peninsula, communities are woven together by palmetto thickets and spartina grass and Gullah-Geechee lore that points to the complicated ancestry of this beautiful dream of a place.

---

DAY
**1**

**CHARLESTON** There's perhaps no better walking city in America than Charleston, where cobblestone streets give way to boutique haberdasheries and verdant parks with sea breezes. Make your residence at THE RESTORATION ON KING, five small dwellings sewed together in the heart of the historic district. Speaking of, roaming the alleyways and one-way streets South of Broad is jasmine-scented voyeurism at its finest. Catch on with TOMMY DEW for a two-hour guided tour. As for the well-deserved raves about the Holy City's restaurants? Here's a trio on Upper King: RODNEY SCOTT'S BBQ for whole-hog divinity; the all-things-Lowcountry seafood pilau at THE GROCERY; and, as a nightcap, a martini and tiny burger at LITTLE JACK'S TAVERN. Trust us, that's the best dessert in town.

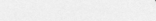

## DAY 2 · HWY 17, BEAUFORT & BLUFFTON

Every road trip begs for that hourlong drive that takes half a day. Here's yours. Cruise the backroads through Johns Island, Wadmalaw and Edisto, then veer up to HIGHWAY 17, all the while soaking in this marshy maritime forest vision. You'll see roadside fruit stands, sweetgrass weavers, crushed-shell driveways and more ghostly oaks than you can count. Stop at MCINTOSH BOOK SHOPPE in Beaufort, a lucky charm of a small town, and pick up a novel by Pat Conroy, the Lowcountry laureate. Before the stars rise, either pitch your surfside tent on HUNTING ISLAND or tuck in for high-end hospitality at PALMETTO BLUFF.

## DAY 3 · SAVANNAH TO CUMBERLAND ISLAND

Savannah could be a trip unto itself, but this time it's a sustenance stop. Hit BACK IN THE DAY BAKERY for what Sean Brock calls the best biscuit he's ever tasted, then head to Cumberland Island. Only 300 visitors are allowed on per day, carried over by ferry from the town of St. Marys. Once there, you'll find wild horses, lazy loggerheads and 18 miles of untouched beaches. Standing sentinel among the scenery is GREYFIELD INN, a Carnegie-built mansion with verandas, antiques and the aura of kingly escape. If you come back ashore, SPEED'S KITCHEN in Shellman Bluff is decidedly unpolished and barely a thousand feet [as the seagull flies] from Blackbeard Creek.

THE RESTORATION ON KING 75 Wentworth St *therestorationhotel.com*

TOMMY DEW'S WALKING HISTORY TOUR *tommydewswalkingtour.com*

RODNEY SCOTT'S BBQ 1011 King St *rodneyscottsbbq.com*

THE GROCERY 4 Cannon St *thegrocerycharleston.com*

LITTLE JACK'S TAVERN 710 King St *littlejackstavern.com*

PALMETTO BLUFF 19 Village Park Square *palmettobluff.com*

BACK IN THE DAY BAKERY 2403 Bull St *backinthedaybakery.com*

GREYFIELD INN 4 N 2nd St *greyfieldinn.com*

SPEED'S KITCHEN 1191 Speeds Kitchen Rd NE

# MEMPHIS AND THE DELTA

*Tennessee, Mississippi*

AVG TEMP
**75 HIGH, 52 LOW**

SUNRISE
**6:03 AM**

SUNSET
**8:13 PM**

RAINY DAYS PER MONTH
**8.5**

TRIP COST
**$950 FOR 2**

SEASONAL ACTIVITIES
**FESTIVALS**

"The Most Southern Place on Earth," according to scholar James Cobb, the Mississippi River Delta posits an enigma. How can the nation's historically poorest region also become its most culturally rich? Birthplace to a wealth of musical, literary, culinary and artistic marvels, the Delta also, arguably, was ground zero for the modern civil rights movement. From city avenues to small-town streets, there is something to the Delta soil, they say. This mud and dirt make miracles happen.

| DAY |
| --- |
| 1 |

**MEMPHIS** A pilgrimage to the NATIONAL CIVIL RIGHTS MUSEUM, located on the site of Martin Luther King Jr.'s assassination, is a must. For lunch, head to the Soulsville neighborhood and THE FOUR WAY Soul Food Restaurant, a seven-decades-old dining room that fed both Dr. King and Elvis. Fill up your plate with turkey and dressing and smothered greens, and save room for pie. Open since 1977, COZY CORNER RESTAURANT is the place for no-frills Memphis barbecue—lunch or dinner—rib plates, sliced-pork sandwiches, smoked Cornish game hens and barbecue spaghetti. Skip Beale Street for the nearby PAULA & RAIFORD'S DISCO, a weekends-only institution where "old school cool" means white leather couches, throbbing funk and soul, and dancing till four in the morning.

| DAY 2 | **CLARKSDALE & GREENWOOD** Travel Highway 61, the Blues Highway, down into the Delta, birthplace of countless legends like John Lee Hooker and Son House. Stop in Leland at the simple but worth-it HIGHWAY 61 BLUES MUSEUM. Pat House, son of the bluesman James "Son" Thomas, plugs into a small amp right there in the glass-cased room of legit ephemera. The only other joint for blues is RED'S LOUNGE, a last-of-kind in Clarksdale. For supper, choose one [or both] of two Delta institutions: DOE'S EAT PLACE in Greenville for tamales and a T-bone, or LUSCO'S in Greenwood for crab-topped pompano in a curtained booth. Rest your bluesy head at the ALLUVIAN HOTEL. |

| DAY 3 | **JACKSON** Begin your visit with a stop on downtown's FARISH STREET, once "the black mecca of Mississippi," according to Geno Lee, owner of the BIG APPLE INN. The inn, a former civil rights headquarters, specializes in Smokes and Ears—griddled smoked sausage and pig ear sandwiches—and also serves up superb cheeseburgers and tamales. End your Delta odyssey at the brand-new MISSISSIPPI CIVIL RIGHTS MUSEUM, the long-awaited chronicle of the state's freedom struggle. Its galleries will leave you simultaneously despondent and inspired, all the while asking, "Where does America go from here?" |

---

NATIONAL CIVIL RIGHTS MUSEUM 450 Mulberry St

THE FOUR WAY 998 Mississippi Blvd *fourwaymemphis.com*

COZY CORNER RESTAURANT 735 N Parkway *cozycorner.com*

PAULA & RAILFORD'S DISCO 14 S Second St *paularaifords.com*

HIGHWAY 61 BLUES MUSEUM 307 N Broad St *highway61blues.com*

RED'S LOUNGE 398 Sunflower Ave

DOE'S EAT PLACE 502 Nelson St *doeseatplace.com*

LUSCO'S 722 Carrollton Ave *luscos.net*

ALLUVIAN HOTEL 318 Howard St *thealluvian.com*

BIG APPLE INN 509 N Farish St

MISSISSIPPI CIVIL RIGHTS MUSEUM 222 North St

# THE MOUNTAIN SOUTH

*Virginia, North Carolina, Tennessee*

AVG TEMP
**68 HIGH, 42 LOW**

SUNRISE
**6:09 AM**

SUNSET
**8:38 PM**

RAINY DAYS PER MONTH
**6**

TRIP COST
**$1400 FOR 2**

SEASONAL ACTIVITIES
**HIKING, CLIMBING, BIKING, SKIING**

At the center of the Appalachian Mountain chain lie its most post-card-perfect peaks: the Blue Ridge Mountains, so called for their blueish tint when seen from a distance, and the Great Smoky Mountains, named for the fog that blankets its crests. These two mountain ranges are flush with as much culture as they are scenic vistas. These lofty lands gave us bluegrass, moonshine and Dolly Parton. Breathe deep, soak up your surroundings and enjoy the cool mountain air.

DAY
**1**

**SHENANDOAH NATIONAL PARK** According to Cherokee lore, Shenandoah means "Beautiful Daughter of the Stars." Fitting for this Blue Ridge utopian wilderness dotted with charming mountain towns like Staunton and Lexington. Make the latter your home base, enjoying GEORGES, the refined Main Street inn, and the RED HEN, a farm-friendly corner restaurant. Take SKYLINE DRIVE, a 105-mile route along the Blue Ridge's spine, where the speed limit maxes out at 35 mph, leaving ample time to crank Old Crow Medicine Show [from Harrisonburg]. In tiny Galax, there's not a better Friday night than bluegrass at THE REX THEATER. The sweet sounds air on WBRF 98.1 FM, if you're roaming the crooked roads at showtime [or streaming from afar].

**DAY 2**

**ASHEVILLE** In the Western Carolina outpost of 89,000 people, there's a woodsy progressiveness in the air. Disc golf duos walk Richmond Hill, string bands busk in Pack Square Park and everyone enjoys having Pisgah National Forest as a backyard. THE GROVE PARK INN, a slope-side hotel built in 1913, isn't quite what F. Scott Fitzgerald experienced, but the history is worth the stay. A bona fide beer town, Asheville houses more breweries per capita than any American city. Stalwarts include WICKED WEED, BURIAL BEER and GREEN MAN. Leave room for smoky delights at BUXTON HALL, Elliott Moss' modern barbecue emporium with whole-hog leanings and veggie sides seasoned with pork drippings. Cap off your night with a glass of bubbly and a Thomas Wolfe novel at BATTERY PARK, a bookstore-slash-Champagne bar.

**DAY 3**

**KNOXVILLE** A literary wellspring—Cormac McCarthy, Alex Haley and James Agee all called it home—Knoxville is, like the best of novels, unassuming but unforgettable. Catch breakfast at the art-filled OLIBEA before heading to the city's visitor center for the BLUE PLATE SPECIAL radio hour, an almost daily live, and free, musical performance—expect bluegrass, country, rockabilly and everything in between. Sojourn to the gem-like OLIVER HOTEL, just down the street from J.C. HOLDWAY, where chef Joseph Lenn honors the cooking of his Appalachian forebears with wood-fired Springer Mountain chicken, cornbread soaked in sorghum and a cornucopia of ramps and fiddlehead ferns.

GEORGES 11 N Main St *thegeorges.com*

RED HEN 11 E Washington St *redhenlex.com*

THE REX THEATER 113 E Grayson St *rextheatergalax.com*

THE GROVE PARK INN 290 Macon Ave *omnihotels.com*

BUXTON HALL 32 Banks Ave *buxtonhall.com*

BATTERY PARK BOOK EXCHANGE 1 Page Ave

OLIBEA 109 S Central St *olibeaoldcity.com*

OLIVER HOTEL 407 Union Ave *theoliverhotel.com*

# BLUEGRASS COUNTRY

*Kentucky*

AVG TEMP
**65 HIGH, 46 LOW**

SUNRISE
**6:28 AM**

SUNSET
**8:58 PM**

RAINY DAYS PER MONTH
**7**

TRIP COST
**$800 FOR 2**

SEASONAL ACTIVITIES
**HORSE RACING, FESTIVALS, CAMPING**

They call Kentucky the Bluegrass State for the green, not blue, bladed lawns transported by colonial settlers. [Let bluegrasses grow to their full height, though, and they bloom tiny blue flowers.] The equestrian and bourbon capital of the world, Kentucky allows visitors to see thoroughbreds graduate from nursery stable to the racetrack and invites whiskey lovers to taste and tour distilleries that specialize in big batched bottles and handcrafted ryes.

---

**DAY 1** **LEXINGTON** Right out of the gate, head to the KENTUCKY HORSE PARK, an equestrian theme park, museum and farm dedicated to the relationship between man and beast. If you're tempted to place a wager, visit the lavish KEENELAND in April or October. If the racetrack isn't your thing, head to the SHAKER VILLAGE OF PLEASANT HILL to experience communal living at its best: sustainable-farming classes, wildlife treks and, of course, backcountry horseback rides. Home to a burgeoning Latino population, the city is affectionately known as "Mexington" and the "Bluegrass Barrio." Don't miss TORTILLERÍA Y TAQUERIA RAMÍREZ, home to one of the nation's top-ranked burritos. Stay at the CAMPBELL HOUSE, where the equestrian-themed décor will get you trotting off to sleep in no time.

<table>
<tr><td>DAY<br>2</td><td>**BOURBON TRAIL** Just west of Lexington, a quartet of bourbon heavyweights cluster around the towns of Lawrenceburg and Frankfort: WOODFORD RESERVE,</td></tr>
</table>

WILD TURKEY, FOUR ROSES and BUFFALO TRACE. All four distilleries are worth a tour and tasting. But save room for at least one of the state's many craft micro-batchers, like OLD POGUE, run by a sixth-generation distilling family making bourbon since 1876. Stay at the majestic BEAUMONT INN in Harrodsburg, winner of a James Beard America's Classic award for its dining room's corn pudding, fried chicken, cured country hams and 70-plus-bottle bourbon selection.

---

<table>
<tr><td>DAY<br>3</td><td>**BARDSTOWN** The Bourbon Trail rolls farther west into delightful Bardstown, Kentucky's second-oldest city. Start your whiskey-soaked dive at the</td></tr>
</table>

BOURBON HERITAGE CENTER, home to Heaven Hill Distillery and an excellent interactive museum. Stop at WILLETT, the state's oldest family-owned and -operated distillery [since 1935] and current cult favorite among serious bourbon drinkers. The antiques-meet-modern rooms of the nearby TALBOTT INN makes a great place to sleep off your weekend, but not before dinner and the chance to raise another glass at the OLD TALBOTT TAVERN, reportedly the world's oldest bourbon bar.

---

KENTUCKY HORSE PARK 4089 Iron Works Pkwy *kyhorsepark.com*

KEENELAND 4201 Versailles Rd *keeneland.com*

SHAKER VILLAGE OF PLEASANT HILL
3501 Lexington Rd *shakervillageky.org*

TORTILLERÍA Y TAQUERIA RAMÍREZ 1429 Alexandria Dr

CAMPBELL HOUSE 1375 S Broadway Rd *curiocollection3.hilton.com*

OLD POGUE 715 Germantown Rd *oldpogue.com*

BEAUMONT INN 638 Beaumont Inn Dr *beaumontinn.com*

TALBOTT INN 107 W Stephen Foster *talbotts.com*

# INTERVIEWS

Fourteen conversations with
locals of note about family history,
vocational pursuits and the
places they call home

# FLORA PAYNE

*BARBECUE LEGEND*

**HORTON AND I** started dating our senior year of high school.

**IN 1972,** he opened the restaurant. He wanted to be his own boss. It was the year I had our first child.

**WHEN I WAS** growing up in Memphis, there weren't as many barbecue places.

**THE FIRST YEAR** was tough, but people at the post office began spreading the word.

**HORTON PASSED AWAY** ten years later, when he was 35. His mother, Emily, and I worked together to take things over.

**I DIDN'T KNOW** a thing about barbecuing.

**WE NEVER ONCE** had an argument. And people have a hard time believing that. She was a special lady.

**OH NO.** You don't put anything on the meat before you put them on the pit.

**THE FAT DRIPPING** on the coals helps the fire, keeps it going, keeps it hot.

**WE COOK** the shoulders all day long. We don't foil anything. We barbecue. We let it get all the smoke it can.

**HORTON'S MOTHER** made the original sauce.

**WE KEEP A POT** on the stove for sandwiches. But you can't boil a hot sauce because it'll make you sneeze all day.

**THE COLESLAW,** when I make it perfect, has a kind of tickling to it.

**NOTHING HAS CHANGED.** The recipes, the sandwiches, the cooking style—everything is the same.

**WHEN YOU HAVE** 46 years, you can perfect something. That and I pray over the food.

**IF HORTON** could see us, he'd be proud. He would think, "Wow. Not her. I can't believe it."

# MATT ARNETT

*ART COLLECTOR AND CURATOR*

**BASEBALL CARDS,** butterflies, Army patches. My dad collected because he used those things to learn. Not because butterflies looked good on the wall.

**HE BEGAN** traveling around the South with the same open eyes.

**WHAT HE FOUND** were lots of people making incredible things. They weren't making things to put them in museums. They weren't trying to make things that white people would find interesting.

**THIS IDEA THAT** something unparalleled in the history of the world was happening in the South didn't smack him on the head until he met Lonnie Holley.

**DRIVING AROUND.** Going to towns. Asking people.

**SOMEBODY** would eventually say, "Oh, there's some weird guy down at the corner over there who's got a bunch of shit in his yard."

**LONNIE** started making art after his niece and nephew died in a house fire and his sister couldn't afford to buy tombstones.

**SUN RA,** Lonnie Holley, Gee's Bend quilters, Thornton Dial and all. There's a geographical reason, a scientific reason why those areas should be so dense with the potential for great art.

**LONNIE HAD THIS ACRE** of land that was just chockablock full of art. And my dad walked up and told him, "What you're doing is as important as anything I've ever seen."

**WE DON'T** use the word folk art.

**FOLK ARTIST,** outsider, visionary. Lonnie says those terms cling to him like an ill-fitted suit.

**THIS PHENOMENON** is like French Impressionism. It had people and artists, but it was a finite thing.

**LONNIE'S ABOUT** the last.

# SANDRA GUTIERREZ

*FOOD WRITER*

**AS A CHILD** in Guatemala, I was extremely shy. I would hide in the kitchen.

**I WAS TOLD THAT** the only way I could hide there was if I cooked something. No idle hands allowed.

**I LIKE TO SAY** I fell in love with the South at the first *y'all.*

**ONE DAY MY HUSBAND** came back from work and said, *"The Cary News* is looking for a food editor. I know you can do this."

**I WROTE AN** article during his lunchtime, he dropped it off and I got a call that afternoon that I'd been hired.

**ONE DISGRUNTLED** reader was very offended that the paper had hired a Mexican to write the Southern-food column.

**I STARTED** asking people if I could come to their kitchens, if they would teach me how to make biscuits, how to make pimiento cheese.

**ONCE YOU SIT** around a table and break bread together, it becomes easier to talk about your differences.

**AROUND 2005,** I noticed this blending of Southern and Latin American flavors in homes and restaurants.

**I'M GOING TO** Crook's Corner and Bill Smith is making sweet potato tamales. What is happening?

**IT'S LIKE A** large tree, and at the roots are African-American cuisine, Native Americans and Europeans.

**SOUTHERN FOOD IS** an amalgamation of cultures that have a shared history of strife and pain and the earth.

**THE WORLD IS** a small place. We've created a lot of divisions. I'm hoping that the table will be the real United Nations.

**FOOD IS** a language of unity.

# GERARD MELANCON

*JOCKEY*

**IF YOU HAVE** a slow horse, you just have a slow horse.

**MY NUMBER ONE** rule: Save ground. A big part of winning is the shortest way around the racetrack.

**THE TOP JOCKEYS** in America actually come from Louisiana.

**WE ALWAYS HAD** bush tracks, little country tracks all over the state. Every Sunday all the horse people went to this track and drank beer and had match races and Calcuttas.

**I'VE SEEN WHERE** they ran horses with no jockey, just with a chicken tied to their back.

**TIE CANS TO THE** horse's tail, the cans make all kind of noise and scare the horse and make him run faster.

**I'M 5'6"** and weigh 114, 115. We eat really healthy, but there's times when we have to eat our crawfish.

**ANYTHING GOES** at the bush tracks. They would get a horse all looped up and run him the fastest.

**I WON** my first race on February 9, 1984.

**I WAS 15** years old. I wasn't scared. I'd ride anything. I'm 100% Cajun. Yessir.

**RIGHT NOW,** I'm right at 4,600 wins.

**BROKEN ARM.** I broke ten ribs. My pelvis, both collarbones. I broke my foot. I've got two compressed fractures in my upper back. Other than that, I've been pretty fortunate.

**NO MONEY,** I didn't have no job. They took my jockey license away. My wife left and moved in with her parents, her and Jansen. I was pretty empty.

**I HAD TO SURRENDER.** That's what it took to make a man of me. It was a long road.

# BRYAN STEVENSON

*LAWYER, SOCIAL JUSTICE ADVOCATE*

**MY GRANDMOTHER'S** name was Victoria Baylor.

**AS A CHILD,** people would come to her home and her father would read the newspaper aloud. She was so proud that her dad, a former slave, was this source of knowledge.

**I CANNOT EXPLAIN** my status as a lawyer without explaining this legacy and this attention to the power of words to liberate, to inform, to shape.

**MY MOTHER WENT** into debt to buy us a set of *World Book Encyclopedia.*

**MY** dad worked in a poultry factory.

**WHEN HE CAME** home from the Korean War, he should have had the privilege under the GI Bill to go to school and to get mortgage assistance. That's how white veterans moved into the middle class.

**BLACK FAMILIES** were denied those opportunities.

**WHEN EMANCIPATION** came for 4 million slave people, there was a promise of property. And the opportunity to develop wealth. That was ultimately denied. And then these skills cultivated during slavery, as farmers and blacksmiths and other blue-collar trades, was undermined by the insecurity created by lynching and racial terrorism.

**MILLIONS OF** black people fled the South to the urban North and West, where they essentially had to start all over again, despite 50 to 100 years of hard work.

**HAVING** proximity to inequality awakens something important for a just society.

**MY FIRST TRIP** to death row as a legal intern, that closeness to condemned people, shaped my thinking. I discovered that I could have an impact by simply being present, by showing up, by being proximate.

**PEOPLE** accused of something are shocked at how quickly they are discarded, even hated. This quick descent can be disorienting.

.................................................

**MY ROLE IS** to respond to the legal challenges, but to also represent the hope of justice.

.................................................

**WE ARE ALL** more than the worst thing that we have done.

.................................................

**JUSTICE** requires that we know the other things that you are. That exploration is how we create a more complete picture of someone's humanity.

.................................................

**WE HAVE NOT** told the truth in our society about slavery and lynching and segregation. When we find the courage to do that, we will be amazed at the power it will release.

.................................................

**IN THE BEGINNING,** the memorial seemed like an odd idea. There were puzzling looks.

.................................................

**WE'VE DOCUMENTED** about 4,300 lynchings. We have the names and dates. We believe there are thousands more.

.................................................

**OUR REPORTS** on slavery and lynching evolved into collecting soil at the sites.

**SOMETHING** concrete, something specific, something particular: Making this legacy of terror tangible is important.

.................................................

**THERE WAS** one black woman doing a collection, alone, digging on a roadside, and this truck drove by and pulled over 100 yards in front of her. A big white man walked up to her and asked her what she was doing.

.................................................

**SHE FELT** compelled and said, "This is where a man was lynched, and I am digging this soil to honor him."

.................................................

**HE STOOD THERE** and she was so nervous. "Would you mind if I helped you?" he said. She offered him the trowel, and he said, "No, no, no. I'll just use my hands."

.................................................

**I FEEL HONORED** to live here and struggle in Montgomery.

.................................................

**BY 1860,** two-thirds of Montgomery County were enslaved black people.

.................................................

**IT'S A PLACE** where the opportunity for restoration and change is rich. And we don't have to fear confronting this history.

**I AM STANDING** on the shoulders of people who frequently had to say, "My head is bloodied but not bowed." The spirits and souls of people like Rosa Parks and Dr. King and those early organizers who fought to end lynching and those emancipated people who found a way to endure hardships.

**THERE WERE THINGS** my grandmother put in my ear that just sat there for a long time. Those things came to life for me when we started this work. Of reflection, of memory, of memorialization. She talked to me about my great-grandfather all the time. She loved her father.

...........................................

**HIS NAME** was James Baylor.

# SID AND ANN MASHBURN

*DESIGNERS AND RETAILERS*

**SID:** Ann's beauty is the light behind her eyes.

**ANN:** I first met Sid in New York when I took the train out to Long Beach for the day. He was on the beach wearing Mardi Gras beads.

**SID:** She was wearing a bikini she'd sewn out of strawberry fabric. It was cute too.

**ANN:** Sid is strong. And he never thinks about the downside. When we first met, I thought, "He's a different kind of cool."

**SID:** I remember the old Mississippi disc jockeys like a baseball roster. That spontaneity of radio, driving town to town, losing one signal and picking up another. It's fantastic.

**ANN:** We looked at 11 cities and it got down to New York and Chicago. Then I said, "How about Atlanta?"

**SID:** I said, "How about fantastic."

**ANN:** We started our shop from scratch with this big, modern, bare space and filled it with furniture we loved from our house.

**SID:** My grandmother had a mercantile when I was a kid called Collier's Cash and Carry in Pelahatchie, Mississippi.

**ANN:** I just adored my grandmother. I make a pumpkin pie out of her old cookbook every Thanksgiving.

**SID:** We're the confidant, the friend, the adviser. We help you to be more comfortable in your own skin.

**ANN:** Confidence is something that grows.

**SID:** My dad had this stash of old watches. Nothing overly special, but he loved them. Wristwatches, pocket watches. That ticking of the watch, it still reminds me of him.

# SARA WARD

*FRESH-SEAFOOD PROPRIETOR*

**MY GREAT-GRANDFATHER** and great-uncle acquired our oyster leases in the 1930s.

.....................................

**TO MAKE** a perfect Apalachicola oyster, you need just the right mixture of saltwater and freshwater.

.....................................

**MY FIVE-YEAR-OLD** niece is obsessed. All she wants is oysters.

.....................................

**I WAS** two when I had my first.

.....................................

**IT'S CALLED 13** Mile Seafood. My grandfather Buddy Ward started it in 1957. It's down toward Indian Pass, 13 miles west of town.

.....................................

**I'VE TRIED** oysters from all over. Apalachicola oysters are salty, briny—not real thick and milky like some others.

.....................................

**NOT TOO FAT,** not too thin.

.....................................

**TOO MUCH** freshwater means too much bacteria. Too much saltwater and you get the conch.

**THEY DRILL** holes into the oysters and kill them. Right now you can go catch 20 pounds of oysters to 60 pounds of conch.

.....................................

**A DECADE AGO,** I'd be on the back dock and my dad, Tommy, would unload 200 bags of oysters a day. Now we're lucky to unload ten a week.

.....................................

**OUR OYSTERS** are $80 a bushel, about 15 dozen. Ten years ago, it was $22.

.....................................

**ASK** where your seafood comes from. It makes a huge difference.

.....................................

**MY** brother TJ has started harvesting farm-raised oysters. They grow in a wild area in baskets.

.....................................

**UNTIL WE** do something to help the bay grow back, that's our only way forward.

.....................................

**TRUST ME,** when I was in high school I was ready to get out of town, where everybody knows everybody. But when it's a family business, it gets in your blood. It's your heritage.

# MARIANNE EAVES

*MASTER DISTILLER*

**I DON'T HAVE** any early memories about bourbon. That's probably unusual for Kentucky.

**OLDHAM COUNTY,** where I grew up, is dry.

**I WAS A SHY KID,** and my mom says I was very cautious.

**I HAVE A** chemical engineering degree from the University of Louisville, and when I finished, the spirits company that makes Woodford Reserve hired me.

**MY BOSS RECOGNIZED** me as being a voracious learner. I raised my hand at every turn. In a few years I became a master taster.

**MY MOM SAYS** I have a good way of garnering confidence and respect, while not being intimidating to men. You've got to balance the fragile male ego!

**MOM REINVENTED** herself in her 40s, going back to college. She's fiercely ambitious, which I hope I inherited from her.

**IT'S RARE TO** get the opportunity to start from scratch, much less on hallowed ground.

**IN 2014,** I was approached by Wes Murry about the restoration of the historic Old Taylor Distillery.

**THE DISTILLERY** site is a treasure, originally built in 1887 by the father of modern bourbon, Colonel E.H. Taylor.

**HE CARED** about integrity above all and understood how to treat guests like royalty.

**I AM THE FIRST** female master distiller in the history of Kentucky bourbon.

**AS MASTER DISTILLER,** I insist on being intimately involved in every single step. Construction, processes, recipes, brand.

**IN FOUR YEARS,** when this bourbon is ready to go, it'll be bottled and it will go on the shelf. And ultimately, I am the one responsible.

# BEN JAFFE

*JAZZ BAND LEADER*

**I GREW** up in the French Quarter, half a block off Bourbon Street.

**I DON'T HAVE** an earliest memory of music. It was just always there.

**ON QUIET** nights I could hear the music coming from Preservation Hall. There was always activity around us, always music, every day.

**THE JAZZ** funerals are a sacred expression of how African-Americans in New Orleans celebrate life and death.

**IT IS** hallowed ground. It's a space, it's an idea, it's a state of being.

**TO FLOURISH,** every great art form, every great cultural tradition, needs a place like Preservation Hall.

**AMERICA NEEDS** New Orleans. It is a cultural center that's important to the entire country. The entire world.

**I LOOK TO THE** pioneers for guidance.

**JELLY ROLL MORTON,** King Oliver, Louis Armstrong, Sidney Bechet. They wrote the music we are still performing today. Where would we be without them?

**IT'S A** delicate balance.

**PRESERVATION HALL** should never become a repertory band. But when you're handed a torch and it's your responsibility to carry that torch forward, you run the risk of becoming a caricature of another time.

**EVERYONE WANTS** to be a horn player in New Orleans.

**THE TUBA** is central to our marching brass band tradition.

**MY FATHER** and Tuba Fats played together in Dejan's Olympia Brass Band.

**JUST ABOUT** any Sunday you can still seek out a parade. It's part of life in New Orleans.

**THE** future of our city matters to the spiritual future of America.

# CEDRIC SMITH

*ARTIST*

**I USED TO** cut hair in Atlanta, and this guy sat in my chair, and I overheard him telling someone else to meet him at his studio.

**I ASKED, "WHAT TYPE** of music do you do?" and he said, "I'm not a musician, I'm an artist."

**HIS NAME WAS** William Tolliver. He was self-taught. His family was poor, from Mississippi, and he had to drop out of school in, like, fifth grade.

**HIS STUDIO LOOKED** like a Neiman Marcus store. Marble floors, baby grand, huge paintings.

**I WENT BACK** to the barbershop and told them, "I'm leaving in a week," and I started painting.

**THERE'S A LACK** of positive imagery of blacks, a whole history of what blacks have contributed to America that we don't hear in school.

**CHUCK D HAS THIS** line: "Most of my heroes don't appear on no stamps."

**MY FIRST SERIES** was positive images of black people on postage stamps, 20 by 30 inches on paper.

**MY GRANDMOTHER** had a neighborhood store that burned down. As kids we'd find old Coca-Cola signs, old food product ads.

**I REMEMBER** thinking, "I don't see nothing on here that's representative of me."

**IT WASN'T UNTIL** I moved to Savannah ten years ago that I realized that there were black Confederate soldiers.

**THIRTEEN** of the 15 jockeys in the first Kentucky Derby were black. I read somewhere that 25 out of every 100 cowboys were black.

**WHAT ELSE** don't I know? That's what I paint.

**WHAT** makes America *America*?

# SHANNON RAVENEL

*EDITOR*

**WHEN I TURNED** eight, two things happened.

**FIRST, IN MY** new school in Charleston, the teacher, Miss Harriet Wilson, read to us constantly.

**SECOND, IT WAS** discovered that I had inherited my mother's severe myopia.

**NEARSIGHTED** kids were to "use their eyes for close-up work as little as possible." My parents bought me a radio to listen to soaps.

**I READ ANYWAY,** by the light of the radio, late into most nights. And I didn't go blind.

**AT HOLLINS,** my mentor told me that he thought I was probably not the fiction writer I thought I wanted to be, but rather a fiction *editor*.

**I LANDED** a job as secretary to the senior editor in Houghton Mifflin's Trade Department. She let me read unsolicited submissions from the "junk pile."

**IN 1977,** I took the job of series editor of *The Best American Short Stories*. This required my reading every story published in all American and Canadian periodicals.

**THAT** was 1,500 stories every year.

**I GREW UP** in racist white South Carolina, where, during summer vacations upstate, an enlightened grandmother led me to understand the evils of racism.

**HER GHOST** was always perched on my shoulder when I was reading those short stories and manuscripts.

**CERTAIN** editorial approaches work better than others.

**I LEARNED** to ask carefully worded questions in the margins of paper manuscripts. "Is this description maybe a bit too long? Can you maybe state it a little bit more directly?"

**MY TWO** all-time favorite short stories are "A Worn Path," by Eudora Welty, and "Sugar Among the Freaks," by Lewis Nordan. Both stories of Mississippi.

. . . . . . . . . . . . . . . . . . . . . . . . . . . . . . . . . . . . . .

I EDITED Pat Conroy's first novel, *The Great Santini*, in 1976.

. . . . . . . . . . . . . . . . . . . . . . . . . . . . . . . . . . . . . .

IMPETUOUS PAT actually drove to St. Louis from Charleston— with his little kids in the car— to hash out some final revisions

. . . . . . . . . . . . . . . . . . . . . . . . . . . . . . . . . . . . . .

HE ALMOST ALWAYS managed to get across his amazing enthusiasm for whatever life had in store for him.

. . . . . . . . . . . . . . . . . . . . . . . . . . . . . . . . . . . . . .

IN 1987, on my way to New York to attend the annual National Book Association, I had a bag full of "little magazines" on the airplane. One of them was *The Mississippi Review*, where I read a story, "Facing the Music," by Larry Brown. It was stunning. The contributor's note said he was a fireman in Oxford.

. . . . . . . . . . . . . . . . . . . . . . . . . . . . . . . . . . . . . .

MANNING the Algonquin booth at the NBA the next day, I noticed a youngish guy in a dark suit, sort of hovering near us.

. . . . . . . . . . . . . . . . . . . . . . . . . . . . . . . . . . . . . .

AFTER A few minutes, he seemed to gather his nerve to come over and ask for me. He introduced himself—Richard Howorth, owner of Square Books in Mississippi.

HE WANTED to tell me about a young writer in Oxford who he, Richard, felt was very talented. I said, "Is he the fireman?" Richard's face registered shock and delight.

. . . . . . . . . . . . . . . . . . . . . . . . . . . . . . . . . . . . . .

AS SOON as I got back to the hotel, I called the number.

. . . . . . . . . . . . . . . . . . . . . . . . . . . . . . . . . . . . . .

LARRY BROWN answered in his low, slow, thick Mississippi accent. I told him I had read "Facing the Music" and wondered if he had any other stories.

. . . . . . . . . . . . . . . . . . . . . . . . . . . . . . . . . . . . . .

"YEAH," he said. "About a hundred." He also had five "good enough" novels. The novels were piled up on a shelf in the shed he'd turned into a writing room.

. . . . . . . . . . . . . . . . . . . . . . . . . . . . . . . . . . . . . .

HE WAS 36 years old, the father of three, a captain at the Oxford Fire Department.

. . . . . . . . . . . . . . . . . . . . . . . . . . . . . . . . . . . . . .

I DREAM of that porch.

. . . . . . . . . . . . . . . . . . . . . . . . . . . . . . . . . . . . . .

WE'D be in Grandmother's cabin by the pond. It was hot, day and night, rain and shine. We favored the porch for both sleeping and reading.

. . . . . . . . . . . . . . . . . . . . . . . . . . . . . . . . . . . . . .

JUST as the crickets started up their evening song, I'd quit and go to sleep just as she turned on her lamp and, for all I knew, read all night long.

# DAVID SHIELDS

*CULINARY HISTORIAN*

**THE OLDEST** surviving vegetables were selected for flavor over thousands of plant generations by various cultures.

**THEY'VE** come down to us embedded with the entire wisdom of peoples.

**I GREW** up in Japan, where my tastes were formed. But it was Virginia, my ancestral stomping ground, where I tasted traditional Southern food for the first time.

**IN THE '90S,** chefs began asking for the restoration of the classic ingredients.

**THE CORN** had become too sweet. There was no Carolina Gold rice. Flavor had become increasingly marginalized.

**A HOLIDAY** meal, a ritual occasion, a communion meal—those moments are an enduring connection to a place. They become part of the matrix of celebration.

**I CAME** out with a list of the vital plants grown in the Lowcountry.

**I CHECKED** germ plasm banks, seed saver's exchanges and original seed catalogs from the 1800s.

**BRADFORD** watermelons were sold for home growing all the way up into the mid-1920s.

**I WROTE A** piece on the "Greatest Tasting Watermelon That Ever Was." Sort of a *Gone With the Wind* piece, tears streaming down my face. Oh how terrible we lost that melon.

**A YOUNG** farmer, eighth generation Bradford descendant, immediately wrote me an email saying that he was growing a patch.

**IT HAD THIS** extraordinary taste, so we revived 19th-century watermelon creations like watermelon molasses, watermelon rind pickle and watermelon brandy.

**WE HAVE** a primordial connection to good flavors.

**WHY TURN** your back on that?

# FRANK RELLE

*PHOTOGRAPHER*

**THERE'S THE SURFACE** of things and then there's the history that's underneath.

**MY FAMILY** first came to Louisiana from Sicily. We grew up on the West Bank.

**AS A** kid, we did a lot of driving around and looking at old homes.

**MY MOM** and dad grew up in houses that were back-to-back. Seven kids on one side, five on the other.

**AS A YOUNG KID,** I spent a ridiculous amount of time looking at birds, and I started collecting exotic, ornate ducks.

**THEY WERE** beautiful and fascinating and strange. All kinds of personality that was displayed in their shape and color.

**THEN I GOT** a microscope. I remember looking at cross sections of plants. There was something about the visual trance that I would describe as soul-opening.

**IN THE '80S,** when the oil crashed in the Gulf, my dad's real estate business went out. They lost the big home, they lost everything.

**I WAS** a teenager, and I began to question the world. And my relationship with nature deepened.

**ECOSYSTEMS** have a way of balancing things out if they're allowed.

**I WAS** waiting tables in the French Quarter when I walked into a gallery of fine photography on Royal Street. The photos were of magnified plants.

**I DIDN'T** take any art classes in school. But I told myself, "I should be a photographer."

**WHAT DREW** me to long-exposure night photographs was the accumulation of time.

**IT'S NOT** just a moment. The light is built up over time. It raises questions.

# FRANK STITT

*CHEF*

**BEING FROM** north Alabama, the South to me has to do with our memories of the small farm.

**THE DEPRESSION** made everyone very sensitive to frugality and stewardship and humble ingredients. People didn't have much cash, but they certainly had a garden.

**MY GRANDAD** plowed with a mule. They farmed strawberries and sweet potatoes and sold eggs from their henhouses.

**RUSTIC** vegetables define Southern food. Butter beans, turnips, mustard greens, tomatoes, sweet potatoes, maybe a little bit of pork.

**MY MOTHER** was regarded by many as the best cook in Cullman.

**SHE MARRIED** my father, and they moved to New York City in the late '40s. They lived in Spanish Harlem.

**OUR TABLE** was very different from my grandparents'. She brought the sophisticated New York style.

**WITH HIGHLANDS,** I wanted really good food without pompousness. A world-class restaurant with integrity and the best ingredients and a lot of love.

**YOU WANT** to be the place that when you walk in the door it feels magical.

**ONE OF OUR** stories is the weary traveler. The person who's had a horrible day and everything has gone wrong and shows up ten minutes after closing time.

**MY** mother almost always had extra food and another place ready in case someone else dropped in.

**THE POINT** is to bring someone something meaningful. To give them an embrace through food.

**A TOMATO** sliced while still warm from the morning sun. Salt, vinegar, a sprig of fresh dill—this was a daily favorite for my mother.

# STORIES

Essays and poetry from
noted Southern voices

# KNOXVILLE: SUMMER OF 1915

*Written by* **JAMES AGEE** | **WE ARE TALKING** now of summer evenings in Knoxville, Tennessee, in the time I lived there so successfully disguised to myself as a child. It was a little bit sort of block, fairly solidly lower middle class, with one or two juts apiece on either side of that. The houses corresponded: middle-sized gracefully fretted wood houses built in the late nineties and early nineteen hundreds, with small front and side and more spacious back yards, and trees in the yards, and porches. These were softwooded trees, poplars, tulip trees, cottonwoods. There were fences around one or two of the houses, but mainly the yards ran into each other with only now and then a low hedge that wasn't doing very well. There were few good friends among the grown people, and they were not enough for the other sort of intimate acquaintance, but everyone nodded and spoke, and even might talk short times, trivially, and at the two extremes of general or the particular, and ordinarily nextdoor neighbors talked quiet when they happened to run into each other, and never paid calls. The men mostly small businessmen, one or two very modestly executives, one or two worked with their hands, most of them clerical, and most of them between and forty-five.

But it is of these evenings, I speak.

Supper was at six and was over by half past. There was still daylight, shining softly and with a tarnish, like the lining of a shell; and the carbon lamps lifted the corners were on in the light, and the locusts were started, and the fire flies were out, and a few frogs were flopping in the dewy grass, by the time the fathers and the children came out. The children ran out first hell bent and yelling those names by which they were known; then the fathers sank out leisurely crossed suspenders, their collars removed and their necks looking tall and shy. The mothers stayed back in the kitchen washing and drying, putting things away, recrossing their traceless footsteps like the lifetime journeys of bees, measuring out the dry cocoa for breakfast. When they came out they had taken off their aprons and their skirts were dampened and they sat in rockers on porches quietly.

It is not of the games children play in the evening that I want to speak now, it is of a contemporaneous atmosphere that has little to do with them: that of fathers of families, each in his space of lawn, his shirt fishlike pale in the unnatural light and his face nearly anonymous, hosing their lawns. The hoses were attached at spigots that stood out of the brick foundations of the houses. The nozzles were variously set but usually so there was a long sweet stream spray, the nozzle wet in the hand, the water trickling the right forearm and peeled-back cuff, and the water whishing out a long loose and low-curved and so gentle a sound. First an insane noise of violence in the nozzle, then the irregular sound of adjustment, then the smoothing into steadiness and a pitch accurately tuned to the size and style of stream as any violin. So many qualities of sound out of one hose: so many choral differences out of those several hoses that were in earshot. Out of any one hose, the almost dead silence of the release, and the short still arch of the separate big drops, silent as a held breath, and only the noise of the flattering noise on leaves and the slapped grass at the fall of each big drop. That, and the intense hiss with the intense stream; that, and that intensity not growing less but growing more quiet and delicate with the turn the nozzle, up to the extreme tender whisper when the water was just a wide of film. Chiefly, though, the hoses were set much alike, in a compromise between distance and tenderness of spray [and quite surely a sense of art behind this compromise, and a quiet deep joy, too real to recognize itself], and the sounds therefore were pitched much alike; pointed by the snorting start of a new hose; decorated by some man playful with the nozzle; left empty, like God by the sparrow's fall, when any single one of them desists: and all, though near alike, of various pitch; and in this unison. These sweet pale streamings in the light out their pallors and their voices all together, mothers hushing their children, the hushing unnaturally prolonged, the men gentle and silent and each snail-like withdrawn into the quietude of what he singly is doing, the urination of huge children stood loosely military against an invisible wall, and gentle happy and peaceful, tasting the mean goodness of their living like the last of their suppers in their mouths; while the locusts carry on this noise of hoses on their much higher and sharper key. The noise of the locust is dry, and it seems not to be rasped or vibrated but urged from him as if through a small orifice by a breath that can never give out. Also there is never one locust but an illusion of at least a thousand. The noise of each locust is pitched in some classic locust range out of which none of them varies more than two full tones: and yet you seem to hear each locust discrete from all the rest, and there is a long, slow, pulse in their noise, like the scarcely defined arch of a long and high set bridge. They are all around in every tree, so that the noise seems to come from nowhere and everywhere at once, from the whole shell heaven, shivering in your flesh and teasing your eardrums, the boldest of all the sounds of night. And yet it is habitual to summer nights, and is of the great order of noises, like the noises of the sea and of the blood her precocious grandchild, which you realize you are hearing only when you catch yourself listening. Meantime from low in the dark, just outside the swaying horizons of the hoses, conveying always grass in the damp of dew and its strong green-black smear of smell, the regular yet spaced noises of the crickets, each a sweet cold silver noise three-noted, like the slipping each time of three matched links of a small chain.

But the men by now, one by one, have silenced their hoses and drained and coiled them. Now only two, and now only one, is left, and you see only ghostlike shirt with the sleeve garters, and sober mystery of his mild face like the lifted face of large cattle enquiring of your presence in a pitchdark pool of meadow; and now he too is gone; and it has become that time of evening when people sit on their porches, rocking gently and talking gently and watching the street and the standing up into their sphere of possession of the trees, of birds hung havens, hangars. People go by; things go by. A horse, drawing a buggy, breaking his hollow iron music on the asphalt; a loud auto; a quiet auto; people in pairs, not in a hurry, scuffling, switching their weight of aestival body, talking casually, the taste hovering over them of vanilla, strawberry, pasteboard and starched milk, the image upon them of lovers and horsemen, squared with clowns in hueless amber. A street car raising its iron moan; stopping, belling and starting; stertorous; rousing and raising again its iron increasing moan and swimming its gold windows and straw seats on past and past and past, the bleak spark crackling and cursing above it like a small malignant spirit set to dog its tracks; the iron whine rises on rising speed; still risen, faints; halts, the faint stinging bell; rises again, still fainter, fainting, lifting, lifts, faints forgone: forgotten. Now is the night one blue dew.

*Now is the night one blue dew, my father has drained, he has*
  *coiled the hose.*
*Low on the length of lawns, a frailing of fire who breathes.*
*Content, silver, like peeps of light, each cricket makes his comment*
  *over and over in the drowned grass.*
*A cold toad thumpily flounders.*
*Within the edges of damp shadows of side yards are hovering*
  *children nearly sick with joy of fear, who watch the unguarding of*
  *a telephone pole.*
*Around white carbon corner lamps bugs of all sizes are lifted elliptic,*
  *solar systems. Big hardshells bruise themselves, assailant: he is fallen*
  *on his back, legs squiggling.*
*Parents on porches: rock and rock: From damp strings morning glories:*
  *hang their ancient faces.*
*The dry and exalted noise of the locusts from all the air at once enchants*
  *my eardrums.*

On the rough wet grass of the back yard my father and mother have spread quilts. We all lie there, my mother, my father, my uncle, my aunt, and I too am lying there. First we were sitting up, then one of us lay down, and then we all lay down, on our stomachs, or on our sides, or on our backs, and they have kept on talking. They are not talking much, and the talk is quiet, of nothing in particular, of nothing at all in particular, of nothing at all. The stars are wide and alive, they seem each like a smile of great sweetness, and they seem very near. All my people are larger bodies than mine, quiet, with voices gentle and meaningless like the voices of sleeping birds. One is an artist, he is living at home. One is a musician, she is living at home. One is my mother who is good to me. One is my father who is good to me. By some chance, here they are, all on this earth; and who shall ever tell the sorrow of being on this earth, lying, on quilts, on the grass, in a summer evening, among the sounds of night. May god bless my people, my uncle, my aunt, my mother, my good father, oh, remember them kindly in their time of trouble; and in the hour of their taking away.

After a little I am taken in and put to bed. Sleep, soft smiling, draws me unto her: and those receive me, who quietly treat me, as one familiar and well-beloved in that home: but will not, oh, will not, not now, not ever; but will not ever tell me who I am.

---

**BORN IN KNOXVILLE, TENNESSEE,** in 1909, poet, playwright and journalist James Agee is most well-known for his documentary classic of sharecropping families in Alabama, *Let Us Now Praise Famous Men*, a collaboration with photographer Walker Evans published in 1941. His essay about Knoxville first appeared in *Partisan Review* in 1938, then as the prologue to his novel *A Death in the Family* in 1957, published two years after the author's death.

# GHOSTS OF GREENWOOD

*Written by* **NIKOLE HANNAH-JONES** | **IN 1947,** my father, along with his mother and older brother, boarded a northbound train in Greenwood, Mississippi. They carried with them nothing but a suitcase stuffed with clothes, a bag of cold chicken and my grandmother's determination that her children—my father was just two years old—would not be doomed to a life of picking cotton in the feudal society that was the Mississippi Delta.

Grandmama, as we called her, settled in Waterloo, Iowa, a stop on the Illinois Central line and a place where thousands of black Mississippians would find work on the railroad or at the Rath meatpacking and John Deere plants. Grandmama took a job familiar to black women of her lot: working for white families as a domestic.

Almost every black person I knew growing up in Waterloo had roots in Mississippi. Mississippi flavored our cuisine, inspired our worship and colored our language. Still, when speaking about the land of their birth, my dad and grandmother talked about family and loved ones, but seldom about the place.

Mississippi was at once my ancestral land and the sinister setting in any number of Hollywood movies, a villain in our national narrative, the place where a black boy named Emmett Till was tossed into the Tallahatchie River with a cotton gin fan around his neck. The only image of Greenwood I got from my family was of my great-grandparents' farm, scenes of chickens and picking peas in the morning sun and my great-grandmother Mary Jane Paul refusing to take any mess. It was only when I got older that I learned my family did not in fact own the farm. Depending on who told the story, my family either leased or share-cropped the land that was, in fact, held by white plantation owners. In reality, the difference mattered little.

And though my parents would load us all in the car every summer to head to a different state for our family vacations, my dad never once took us to the state of his birth. Not for family reunions or funerals. Not for graduations or holidays. My father and grandmother both passed away without ever taking me to see their home.

As the nation prepared to mark the 50th anniversary of Freedom Summer—that violent and heady 10 weeks during which Northern volunteers joined forces with Southern activists in Mississippi, all working to meaningfully enfranchise black residents—I felt pulled to finally visit this place that ran in my blood but that I had never seen. At the age of 38, I visited Mississippi for the first time.

My 87-year-old great-aunt, Charlotte Frost, who had followed my grandma to Waterloo, happened to be visiting a granddaughter in Jackson at the same time I planned my trip. I picked up Aunt Charlotte and we headed north on U.S. 49 toward Greenwood, into the heart of the Delta and Freedom Summer's ground zero.

The Mississippi Delta, named after the river that gives it life, stretches 200 miles long and 60 miles wide, covering 19 counties in the Magnolia State. The ebb and flow of the mighty river left behind some of the richest soil on the face of the earth [topsoil here can reach more than 60 feet deep]. This dark, fertile land, and the riches it could produce for the white people who owned almost all of it, would also make Mississippi one of the most dangerous places in the country to be black.

As we drove, I tried to get Aunt Charlotte to open up about what it was like coming of age in a black family in the Delta. It was here, after all, that life for black people was so grim that it spawned the blues.

But Aunt Charlotte, peering out at the road through round glasses perpetually clinging to the end of her nose, said she never had any problems with white people, that they had respected her family and hadn't done much to bother them. And then Charlotte went on to talk about the good school she went to in town and all the crops her family grew.

It was a familiar take. She and another great-aunt in Waterloo are the last of my Grandmama's siblings, and I had tried before to get their stories but had been met with a resistance to talking about the ugliness of Jim Crow Mississippi. I never push too hard at this gauzy version, because I know that women like my great-aunts—they pride themselves in their durable dignity, dress to nines, don't use vulgar language and keep impeccable homes with plastic-wrapped sofas—have no desire to speak of the daily degradations they'd faced at the height of Jim Crow.

A wooden sign coated in brown paint announced our arrival: *Welcome to Greenwood, Cotton Capital of the World.*

But it was clear from the rows of lanky corn stretched out before the sign—not exactly squat June cotton—that the greeting's boast was mere nostalgia.

We first headed to the Little Zion Missionary Baptist Church just outside of town. The plain, white structure was where our family worshipped. My great-grandmother and great-grandfather Mary Jane and Percy Paul, part of the first generation born out of slavery, are buried in the overgrown cemetery, with its haphazardly placed tombstones. It turns out that this church is the one featured in the movie *The Help*, the place where the maids went to worship. I would come to learn that though the movie is set in Jackson, it was mostly filmed in Greenwood because the town seemed largely frozen in time. Its building and homes, and in some ways its culture, form a kind of time capsule of the era when cotton was king.

**THIS DARK, FERTILE LAND, AND THE RICHES IT COULD PRODUCE FOR THE WHITE PEOPLE WHO OWNED ALMOST ALL OF IT, WOULD ALSO MAKE MISSISSIPPI ONE OF THE MOST DANGEROUS PLACES IN THE COUNTRY TO BE BLACK.**

According to Aunt Charlotte, the church used to be a part of the Whittington Plantation, the white landowners having built it for the black sharecroppers. It's still surrounded by crops, and Aunt Charlotte, stooped over her cane, pointed to a distant spot in the fields, saying their house, the house where my great-grandmother helped deliver my father, once stood there on the Whittington lands. I soon learned that nearly every black person here came from a family attached through labor [and sometimes blood] to white families and to plantations with names like "Star of the West."

It was dusk, and the Delta heat settled about my shoulders like a wool blanket. Heavy and uncomfortable, it made my notebook paper fall limp and my ink stop flowing. Gnats and mosquitoes swarmed my legs. Aunt Charlotte, wrapped in a memory, paused to listen to an owl hooting a melancholy warning.

"The old people would say someone is going to die," she said.

Located in Leflore County, my dad's hometown took its name from Greenwood LeFlore, the last Choctaw Indian chief, who signed over much of the tribe's land for an Oklahoma reservation while he himself lived lavishly on 15,000 acres of Delta land that he worked with some 400 enslaved black laborers.

The Civil War, of course, left much of the South crippled, but not long after Reconstruction, Greenwood boomed. While white politicians in Jackson led the South in stripping black residents of their elected offices and newly guaranteed citizenship rights, white plantation owners rebuilt the levees on the flood-prone and swampy Delta. Cotton once again stretched as far as the eye could see, and Greenwood took its place as one of the cotton capitals of the world.

But this boom was made possible only by a reconstituted slavery, a system of coerced labor known as sharecropping. Vagrancy laws were passed, making it illegal for black people to stand around "idle." Often the only defense was to prove one was in the employ of a white person.

White Mississippians, outnumbered by the African-Americans needed to work the land, implemented a violent and absolute form of social control. The nation's most heavily black state, Mississippi lynched more black people between 1882 and 1968 than any state in the country.

Greenwood's Yazoo River is formed by the meeting of the Tallahatchie and Yalobusha rivers, and as we crossed the Yazoo River and headed to the heart of Greenwood, the ghosts of Mississippi grew close, and Aunt Charlotte finally loosened.

Aunt Charlotte told me that she was baptized in the Tallahatchie. She went on to speak of another river baptism, into the perils of the Delta's color line.

She said her brother Milton—my dad's namesake—and a cousin had once committed the sin of walking through a white neighborhood for a reason other than to simply go to work. Two white teenagers in a car gave chase, trying to run them down. Her brother and cousin were forced to jump into the murky river to escape. They returned home, muddy and wet, chests heaving from panic and exertion. Her mother, she said, was livid with fear.

"They got a hard scolding," Aunt Charlotte said. "She said, 'You're going to get yourself killed.'"

We drove past the regal white courthouse, with its requisite Confederate monument standing guard out front. Aunt Charlotte told of another brother running home, chest heaving. A cousin who leased farmland from a white plantation owner had the gall to stand up to a white overseer who didn't like him having taken a rest. Everyone knew that simply asserting one's manhood could get a man strung from a tree, so her brother raced to get my great-grandfather to help guard his cousin against the lynching mob.

"My daddy grabbed his Winchester and rifle and his .38 long-nose pistol," Aunt Charlotte said, and he headed to the cousin's house to keep vigil. This was a well-practiced event: Family members often gathered arms to protect a loved one following a social breach, usually keeping watch until the loved one could be whisked out of town, almost always to the North.

"They usually had to leave before nightfall or the lynching mob would come," Aunt Charlotte said quietly. The lynching mob did not come that night, but Aunt Charlotte never forgot the fear. That fright was as routine among black people in the Delta as heading to church on Sunday.

It was just a few miles outside of town, after all, where they found the body of Emmett Till. The tossing of black bodies into the muddy rivers for breaching the social order wasn't unusual. The only reason people across the nation knew Till's name was that his mother insisted on an open casket and allowed the ghastly photos of his bloated and mutilated corpse to be published in the nation's leading black publications.

It was eerie being down here where it happened, just a few miles from where my dad grew up, and realizing how easily he could have been Till. We somehow convince ourselves that this is ancient history. But I am not even 40, and my dad was but four years younger than Emmett Till. Like my dad, Till's mother had also left as one of hundreds of thousands of black Mississippians who fled their homeland during the Great Migration.

Mamie Till ended up in Chicago and, like my Grandmama, sent her son back down South during the summer months. My dad even shared Emmett Till's light eyes, as well as that bravado that came from living in the North—that bravado that brought out the worst in white Southerners. One of my Dad's cousins told me that when he came back to Greenwood for the summers, my dad liked "progueing," a local word for strutting around and being seen. He told me my great-grandparents kept Dad close.

Fear and economic exploitation were the twin elements that defined the Delta. Both were made possible by the complete disenfranchisement of the majority black population. North Greenwood, with its wide, tree-lined avenues and *Gone With the Wind* mansions, once prompted the U.S. Chambers of Commerce to name its main thoroughfare one of the nation's most beautiful streets. Divided from the rest of the town by the Yazoo River, it showcased the vast material wealth under King Cotton. The shotgun shacks in southeast Greenwood, with its unpaved roads and lightless blocks at the time, revealed who paid the price for that wealth.

"You had to sharecrop, you couldn't sell your own cotton, you had to go to them," the white people, "for everything," the Reverend Willie Blue, a Mississippi native who took part in Freedom Summer, told me. "You didn't make anything, you were always in the hole and at the end of the year there was never anything left. They controlled your life. It was the same thing as being a slave."

An entire family could work all year—children as young as two had to go to the fields—and walk away with $100. Even though other Southern states embraced mechanization, Mississippi avoided it. As a local historian told me, it was cheaper to "pay" sharecroppers.

White people in Greenwood made up 33 percent of the population but owned 90 percent of the land. Just 2 percent of eligible black voters were registered. Black residents held not a single elected office. In 1964, 10 years after the Supreme Court's *Brown v. Board of Education* decision, Mississippi was the only state in the country where not a single black child attended a school with a white child.

Still, black Mississippians weren't just cowering in fear, awaiting saviors from the North.

In 1954, a young man named Medgar Evers attempted, without success, to integrate the University of Mississippi Law School. That same year, the NAACP named him Mississippi's first field officer, and he spent the next decade enduring death threats and violence as he tried to register black voters.

Black Mississippians attempted to desegregate schools and lunch counters, movie theaters and swimming pools. But sit-ins to eat at an integrated restaurant were one thing. Pushing to access the vote in such a heavily black region was something else.

"If we get the right to vote, we become captains of our own ship," Blue told me. "I believed that then, I believe that now." He added: "You are not a first-class citizen if you are not registered to vote. That's the backbone of being American. The vote is the perfect example of free speech."

Hank Klibanoff, a journalist and co-author of the book *The Race Beat: The Press, the Civil Rights Struggle, and the Awakening of a Nation*, explained to me the promise and threat of black enfranchisement. Not only did voter registration lead to political representation, Klibanoff said, but it also determined who sat on juries. "You become instrumental in ensuring criminal justice is effective and fair," Klibanoff said. Access to the vote "really made it possible for blacks to finally get justice in the courts, not just criminal but civil as well."

White Mississippians understood this as clearly as anyone. The toll on black bodies during the effort to ensure voting rights is, for people of my generation, inconceivable. In the years leading up to Freedom Summer, black Mississippians agitating for civil rights were beaten by mobs, castrated, dragged behind cars with ropes, bombed, jailed, beaten with belts and whips by their jailers, shot at and strung with 100 pounds of rocks and sunk to the bottom of the river. None of this was done in secret: Among the murderers was a state legislator and a county sheriff.

"We have unintentionally reduced racial discrimination to images of white and colored water fountains. And in that context, what passes for violence is somebody pouring mustard on top of a civil rights demonstrator at a lunch counter, when in fact it was open season on blacks," Klibanoff said. "They could be killed just indiscriminately and with impunity. And I don't mean, now and then, but I mean fairly regularly."

And this is where it's easy to cast Mississippi as a grotesque outlier, and to feel a certain smugness about how, as the civil rights veterans put it at the time, Freedom Summer was about making Mississippi part of the rest of America. But the rest of America—exemplified by the federal government—knew what was happening in Mississippi. We knew that Mississippi was nearly half black but had no black representatives in Congress or anywhere, from state government on down. We knew black Mississippians were being denied their citizenship rights and being murdered for having the audacity to demand them. Despite obvious voter intimidation and political assassinations, the FBI operated no field office there. We knew, and we looked away.

Every day, ordinary Mississippians battled on.


Reverend Blue joined the Mississippi civil rights movement in 1963. Blue, who returned home to Tallahatchie County after a stint in the Navy, had been getting pressure from whites to find work on a plantation or to get out of town. Blue instead headed to Greenwood, where he hooked up with Bob Moses.

Moses, a Harvard-educated New Yorker, had come to Mississippi in 1961 to work on voter registration for the Student Nonviolent Coordinating Committee, known as SNCC. Greenwood was, according to SNCC documents, a "hard core resistance area." Moses set up SNCC's headquarters in Greenwood—those headquarters would be bombed, burned down and shot up—and Blue's first task was to pick up Harry Belafonte and Sidney Poitier, who were coming to Greenwood to offer their support.

Blue, still green as an activist, arrived at the airport only to encounter a cadre of armed Klan members. The two-car delegation picked up their Hollywood guests, and Blue, who was driving the second car, soon found himself in a high-speed chase with the Klan. The Klan backed off once the party made it to the black part of Greenwood. Laughing ruefully today, Blue said he didn't find out until later that Poitier and Belafonte had been carrying tens of thousands of dollars in cash to help the voting rights effort.

Outside of town, on a car-strewn lot tucked between cotton fields, I met with Silas McGhee, whose family, led by his mother, Laura, began fighting Jim Crow long before Freedom Summer. They paid a heavy price. McGhee doesn't much like to talk about those times. I couldn't get him to sit for an interview. All he would say was that he was no hero, that he had just done what he was supposed to do. McGhee had been jailed and beaten more times than he could count for trying to desegregate downtown businesses and help register black voters.

But the sunken set of his jaw told the story he would not. At the height of the Mississippi civil rights struggle, a white man pulled up in a car and shot McGhee in his face when McGhee was sitting outside of a Greenwood restaurant. The bullet barreled through his mouth, taking his front teeth with it. Blue, who was with McGhee at the time, told me, and McGhee confirmed, that the shooter was Byron De La Beckwith—the Klansman who killed Medgar Evers. I could find no record to prove or disprove it.

As I left McGhee working on a tractor in his yard, I thought of how all but one of Grandmama's seven siblings who survived into adulthood left Mississippi in their youth. They sacrificed a great deal in seeking a better life for their families. But it was in talking to people like Blue and McGhee that I realized what an act of defiance it was to have been a black Mississippian and to have simply stayed put. Staying to change this state might well have been the greatest sacrifice.

So, no, black Mississippians hadn't been waiting for saviors—white or otherwise—from outside. But they certainly welcomed them for the national attention they would bring.

Moses—who civil rights veterans say was blessed with the right name—is largely considered the mastermind behind Freedom Summer. When I spoke with him over the phone, he brushed off the credit.

Moses had been tested in Mississippi's fire. He'd been beaten in the back of the head with the butt of a knife by the cousin of a local sheriff, he'd been shot at, he'd been jailed and beaten some more. Speaking to me from Jackson, where he'd traveled for a Freedom Summer commemoration, Moses called what they were doing back in the 1960s "guerrilla warfare." They were sniping at the system while being housed and protected by the local community.

"It was the only time in my life where I could any time of night go and knock on a door, and they were going to provide a bed for me to sleep in, food to eat and watch my back," he said of the network of local black Mississippians who sheltered civil rights workers. "You had in that community people who were willing to take a stand even though they knew what they were doing would enrage white folks."

In 1963, Medgar Evers joined the long list of racial assassination victims. De La Beckwith followed Evers home and shot Evers through the heart with a rifle. Evers was carrying a box of T-shirts proclaiming "Jim Crow Must Go." Mississippi governor Ross Barnett visited De La Beckwith during his trial. Two all-white juries deadlocked and Evers' killer would live free and in the open until 1994, when he was finally brought to justice.

Moses said the killing of Evers was the turning point.

Two years of voter efforts in Greenwood had led to fewer than 30 black registrations but plenty of shootings, beatings, bombings and arrests. A 1963 memo written by Bob Moses stated:

*We have learned the following:*

*1. It is not possible to for us to register Negroes in Mississippi ...*

*2. All direct action campaigns for integration have had their backs broken ...*

He went on: "The Mississippi monolith has successfully survived the Freedom Rides, James Meredith at Ole Miss, and the assassination of Medgar Evers, without substantive change. ... The only attack worth making is an attack aimed at the overthrow of the existing political structure of the state."

It was time to up the ante. Reporters for the mainstream press had largely bought white Mississippians' protestations that black Mississippians just didn't care to vote. The idea was somehow to provoke the federal government to act.

So the notion was hatched to recruit college students from across the country who would converge on the state for 10 weeks, setting up Freedom Schools and registering black voters. The goal: To register enough disenfranchised black voters to challenge the all-white Democratic delegation at the national convention in Atlantic City, New Jersey, and instead seat the biracial Mississippi Freedom Democratic Party.

To work, the organizers calculated, a significant number of the student volunteers needed to be white.

"We know what they bring with them are the eyes of the country," Moses told me. "The country is able to see through their eyes what they weren't able to see through ours."

We both grew silent on the line, for just a moment, letting those words sink in.

Of course, most everyone knows what happened next. As Freedom Summer began, three civil rights workers—Michael Schwerner and Andrew Goodman, two white Northerners; and James Earl Chaney, a black Mississippian—disappeared in Mississippi. Black Mississippians immediately understood what that meant.

"There is no kidnapping in Mississippi," Reverend Blue reminded me. "We knew they were dead."

But the murders of those two white men changed everything. "These were not just white folks," they were "America's finest, America's futures," Reverend Blue said. "Goodman's richer than whipped cream. He wasn't supposed to die in Vietnam, he sure wasn't supposed to die in Mississippi. When America's brightest are murdered for doing something fundamentally American, suddenly the world knows about Mississippi. It was another nail in the segregated coffin."

The federal government swarmed Mississippi. The FBI opened an office there for the first time in two decades. The nation's eyes wound up riveted on a place that many felt had existed outside the laws of the land. And as law enforcement dragged rivers searching for the missing civil rights workers, they found at least nine bodies of black men who'd disappeared well before. The beatings, bombings and jailings of Freedom Summer volunteers and local Mississippians determined to exercise democracy continued all summer.

In the end, despite all the attention to the three slain civil rights workers, and the gathering of tens of thousands of signatures of black Mississippians who wanted to vote but couldn't, the Mississippi Freedom Democratic Party did not unseat Mississippi's all-white delegation. Their efforts were squashed by the very man who would pass the most sweeping civil rights legislation since Reconstruction, President Lyndon Baines Johnson. Freedom Summer volunteers and organizers left Atlantic City dejected.

So, what then, was Freedom Summer's legacy—not just in some grand national narrative but right here in the Delta as well?

I picked Aunt Charlotte up from the Hampton Inn on the edge of town, and we headed to Mississippi Avenue, where my cousin Lawrence Paul lives. I'd never met Lawrence, but when I had called a few days earlier and introduced myself as a relative from up North and told him of my visit, he'd asked, "Whose daughter are you again?" When I told him Milton's, he let out a hearty laugh.

"Ol' cat-eyed Milton?" he asked. "We used to be real close. Call me when you get here and come on by."

Lawrence lives in a neighborhood of stately brick homes and bungalows. Greenwood is marked by severe residential segregation, and Lawrence explained that the neighborhood used to be all white. But once the first black people moved in, every last one of the white residents moved out. Now it is home to Greenwood's small black middle class, a collection of civil servants, educators and entrepreneurs.

Lawrence is the grandson of my Grandmama's brother, the only sibling who hadn't gone North. Lawrence was 14 when Freedom Summer happened. Sitting in front of the air conditioner and sweating under a blue baseball cap, he smiled at the memory.

"To me, I am not going to use the word 'revolutionary'—but it felt good knowing we were part of something," Lawrence said. "It was a hurting thing to be a youngster. Seeing the way the police did our parents, it was brutality. You had a law for white and a law for black. You see an all-white government, all-white police force, all-white everything."

**"OUR PEOPLE WERE STILL SUFFERING AND WE WANTED A PIECE OF THE PIE. THE ONLY WAY TO GET IT WAS TO FIGHT."**

Lawrence repeated the stories of daily fear, of not stepping off a sidewalk fast enough, or appearing too smart or too proud, and the instant wrath it could bring. As a young boy, he said, he'd learned to differentiate a police car without even having to turn around. Just the sound it made gave it away.

"I can still hear it," he said. "They'd pull alongside us and we'd say, 'Yes, sir, yes sir.' We'd fake it."

Fake what, I asked.

"Deference."

Aunt Charlotte, who'd been sitting in the chair listening, spoke up. "My dad would always say, 'I'm a man. How old do I have to be to be a man?'"

Outside of the watchful eyes of his parents, Lawrence went to organizing meetings held at the Elks Lodge; he marched to the courthouse and picketed for voting rights that he was too young to exercise. "Our people were too afraid to march, so we did it for them," he said proudly.

Lawrence didn't mind at all the white Northerners who had often been portrayed in news media as the face of the movement that summer.

"White people were the key to it," he said. "They were a major part of the change."

It reminded me of something Reverend Blue had said: "This movement belonged to all of us."

At the end of Freedom Summer, most of the volunteers left. And they took with them the nation's attention. Life remained hard for those left behind. Churches and homes continued to be bombed. Despite the passage a year later of the Voting Rights Act, white Mississippians continued to violently fight efforts to register black voters and gain black political power.

In fact, two years after Freedom Summer, in 1966, James Meredith, the man who integrated Ole Miss, was shot in Mississippi as he tried to complete a "March Against Fear." Stokely Carmichael, a SNCC veteran, tried to complete Meredith's march but wound up jailed in Greenwood, marking his 27th arrest in the fight for civil rights. The lack of progress had taken a physical and emotional toll on Carmichael and others who'd spent years in the trenches. It was in Greenwood that a fiery Carmichael gave his first "Black Power" speech, fracturing the movement into those who wanted to continue with a nonviolent agenda and those who decided that if someone hit at them, they were going to hit back.

Despite the passion of Freedom Summer, Lawrence explained, it seemed that little had changed when it was over. "After Freedom Summer, for me, it was still the same," he said, wiping at his brow with a white washrag. "It was something forced upon them. It didn't happen fast."

Changes did come, of course, but achingly slowly. Shortly after the passage of the Voting Rights Act, David Jordan, the son of a sharecropper on the same Whittington Plantation where my family worked, who'd earned degrees from Mississippi Valley State and the University of Wyoming and become a science teacher, established the Greenwood Voters League to register black voters and help them wield the political power their numbers should have brought. But by

1977, a full decade after Freedom Summer, Greenwood's governance remained lily-white. That year, Jordan sued the city under the Voting Rights Act and won the suit eight years later. While the lawsuit against Greenwood worked its way through the courts, Jordan sued again, this time to change the way the state drew legislative districts, which had continued to ensure the election of white candidates. Jordan won there as well, leading to the 1984 election of Mississippi's first black congressman since Reconstruction.

"Our people were still suffering and we wanted a piece of the pie," Jordan said. "The only way to get it was to fight."

The following year, in 1985, Jordan ran for the newly formed City Council and became Greenwood's first black city councilman.

For his efforts, Jordan's had his life threatened, his property vandalized and, in 2011, his house shot. Today, Greenwood's City Council has a black majority. It has a black fire chief. It has had a black mayor and chief of police. Jordan himself holds two elected positions; he's a city councilman and a state senator. Sitting in the City Council chambers, he noted that Mississippi can now boast the most black elected officials of any state in the Union. Through the window at his back, the stars and bars of the Confederacy, enshrined on the Mississippi state flag, fluttered in the wind.

"Freedom Summer baptized Mississippi as part of the nation," Moses said. "It was no longer a rule unto itself."

Still, the limitations of Freedom Summer and the Mississippi civil rights movement stand in stark relief. Mississippi remains the nation's most heavily black state, and also its poorest. Political power has not brought economic power.

Greenwood, the town that bet everything on King Cotton, has suffered from cotton's demise. But the suffering has not been borne evenly. Entire sections of the once-thriving city center are pocked with vacant storefronts and empty streets. And yet a few blocks over, a bustling collection of shops cater to the tourists and other well-off vacationers and locals drawn to the luxury Alluvian hotel and spa.

In the past, seeking to hoard all the cheap black labor for their cotton fields, the city's white elite fought to keep other industries away. Today, then, the town struggles to draw any industry whatsoever.

Meanwhile, cotton fields have been converted to much less labor-intensive corn and soybean crops. Those crops have kept many white families well-off, comfortable in their sprawling mansions. North Greenwood, where nearly all the city's white residents live, has almost no poverty to speak of.

But today, well over a third of Greenwood's black residents live below the poverty line. The lack of industry and loss of agricultural work have left many simply jobless. Across the tracks, the historic all-black Baptist Town is a collection of dilapidated shotgun homes. Those battered and leaning homes, first constructed to house sharecroppers, cannot possibly look any better now than they did during Jim Crow. In significant parts of this community, the median family income falls below $10,000 a year. Its residents are so generationally impoverished that the community is eagerly awaiting two dozen tiny cottages left over from Hurricane Katrina.

Both Moses and Blue said that while a small number of black Mississippians have been able to gain wealth and power, distressingly high numbers still remain mired in grinding poverty. "Those that gained the most from the movement don't want to trouble the water," Blue told me. "They are doing so good while most of us are doing so much worse. Integration comes with finance. I can't go to the country club—not because I am black, but because I don't have money. I think that's the failure. The lack of financial power."

Many who risked their lives for the struggle faced retribution once the cameras went away and the volunteers went home. They talked of being blackballed from jobs, loans, opportunity. Many of them live on Social Security and scrape by.

The younger generation, those for whom Freedom Summer is their inheritance, are in obvious ways better off than those before them. Yet they still can feel trapped. I met 23-year-old Evonna Lucas at the city's convention and visitors bureau. An outspoken bookworm fascinated by history, she reminded me of myself when I was her age.

Evonna remembers clearly when she first confronted Greenwood's invisible color line. She was in fourth grade and her mother had sent her to the only Greenwood public school that is majority white. Her best friend was a little white girl named Sarah, and Sarah was having a birthday party. "We were so excited. Then she came one day and said, 'My momma said I can't invite black kids to my birthday,'" Evonna told me. "I still remember her head hanging down. She was in fourth grade and couldn't look me in the eye. That's when I realized I was different."

I grew up in Iowa, yet have a story like that of my own. The only difference is I was welcomed at my white friends' homes; it's just that their parents didn't want them coming to mine. I guess Moses was right when he told me that the success of Freedom Summer was it "made Mississippi, for better or for worse, the same as the rest of the country."

Evonna graduated from historically black Mississippi Valley State University last year with a degree in communications. She returned home and, finding she couldn't get a job in her field, took what she could get, making minimum wage before landing the job at the visitors bureau. She likes it, but she wants more. She worries that can't happen unless she leaves. What's possible when you live in the Delta, she told me, can seem so small.

"I won't say Freedom Summer didn't achieve anything, because look at me, I am sitting here in an office that never had a black person," she said. "We had a black mayor, my doctors are black. But our kids still don't get the best education and the system is handicapping them. What's it all for?"

And later that night, I saw the old Mississippi peeking through the veneer.


When I drove my great-aunt back to Jackson, she had rather casually pointed at a restaurant named Lusco's that had been in that exact location when she was a child. Of course, as a child she'd been barred from eating there. I immediately decided that I would eat there that night upon my return.

Lusco's was founded in 1921 by Italian immigrants who solidified their assimilation process by banning black diners. Five generations later, the restaurant is still owned by the same family. And its inside looks much as it did during Freedom Summer. The same linoleum, though faded and peeling. The same soda fountain stools, though the soda fountain is long gone.

The clientele is nearly all white, and since Lusco's is but a few blocks from Baptist Town, a black security guard stands outside, opening the door for every patron coming in and out and walking them the few feet to their car.

I stood outside and talked to the hostess who'd stepped outside for a smoke. She was part of that Lusco fifth generation. "Our customers don't like change," she told me, complaining about the restaurant's dated interior.

As I talked to her, a boisterous older white couple, probably in their 70s, came out. The woman was charming and seemed used to attention. I was told that everyone simply refers to her as "Mrs. Greenwood." She was carrying a bottle of wine under her arm and casually declared that she'd already finished one. Mrs. Greenwood asked me and the photographer with me where we were from.

Just then, two young black men walked by. Quietly, eyes down, they headed to the store at the corner. It was steamy out, and one was shirtless. Mrs. Greenwood's eyes followed them, and a sneer curled her lips.

"That's what you call our 'local color,'" she said. The last word, which she pronounced "CAH-la," sounded mean and hard in my ears. The photographer and I exchanged looks but said nothing. Perhaps I blanched, because Mrs. Greenwood tried to recover.

"I'm not being ugly," she said. "It's not safe here." She scurried to the beige town car where her husband was waiting and they drove off, I imagined to their home across the Yazoo River.

I went back to my hotel room and wrote in my notes, "The Delta can be devastating."

Still, I couldn't help but recall that same morning when a young white man saw Aunt Charlotte trying to get into her car and rushed over to her, opened the door and then solicitously held her purse while she pulled her arthritic legs into the car. He had called her "ma'am" and wished her a nice day.

I left Greenwood a few days later. At the Jackson Airport, which is now called Jackson-Medgar Wiley Evers International Airport, sits a little portico right at the check-in counters. It's dedicated to Evers and traces some of the key moments in Mississippi's struggle for civil rights. At the center in the back stands a bronze statue of a little white girl with her arm thrown around the shoulder of a little black girl.

On the inscription it said: *Reconciliation: a work in progress.*

---

**NIKOLE HANNAH-JONES** is an investigate reporter at *The New York Times Magazine*. Her work, which largely focuses on issues of racial injustice, has appeared in ProPublica, *The Atlantic* and *Essence,* among others. In 2016, Hannah-Jones co-founded the Ida B. Wells Society for Investigative Reporting, whose aim is to train, mentor and increase the number of reporters of color. A year later, she earned a MacArthur "Genius Grant" for her reporting on school segregation. This piece was originally published by ProPublica in July 2014 and is reprinted with permission.

# REAL PLACES IN ALABAMA

*Written by* **DANIEL WALLACE** | **I CREATED A TOWN.** I didn't establish it, or sink a single nail: I'm an avid indoorsman, always have been. I created it the way God used to create things, with words. I know how that sounds. Comparing yourself to God never comes off well, but trust me, in every other way God and I could not be more different. It's just that in this case we're a match: I invented the idea of a place on the page, and, voilà, now it exists. It has a longitude and latitude. You can go there. Enterprise, Warrior, Black Bottom, Vestavia, Opp, Fairhope, Blue Eye, Homewood, Smoke Rise, Damascus, Burnt Corn, Bacon Level, Mountain Brook—all real names of real places in my home state of Alabama. But Spectre is the name of the town I made with words.

I invented Spectre, or Specter, on page 144 of my first novel, *Big Fish:*

"[One day Edward Bloom] finds himself, quite by accident, stuck. In a little town called Specter. Specter, a town somewhere in Alabama or Mississippi or Georgia. Stuck there because his car has broken down ... Specter, not surprisingly, turns out to be a beautiful little town full of small white houses, porches and swings, beneath trees as big as all time to give them shade." Long story short: Edward Bloom falls in love with the town and decides to buy it, and this is exactly what he does.

That was just in a book, though. Now Spectre is on the map, literally, near Montgomery. It's 84 miles from Birmingham, where I grew up, and 552 miles from where I live now, in Chapel Hill, North Carolina. Just the idea that Spectre is a certain number of miles from anywhere you can think of—2,097 miles from Santa Monica, California!—makes me feel as though I've really made a difference. It's one of the most consequential things I've ever done. To put it in context: I've published six novels, dozens of stories and essays, and two children's books. But Spectre is my only town.

[Note: They call it an abandoned movie set, but now you know it's so much more.]

Cullman, Alabama, is a town I did not create. German Lutherans did that, way back in the middle of the 19th century. Decades later, though, my father was born there, and when he came of age, he left, because, as he told me later, and told me often, "I didn't want to be a big fish in a little pond." He needed an ocean, and he found one.

His parents, my grandparents, stayed behind, and we'd visit them in Cullman two or three times a year. I got to know the town pretty well. It was simple and tiny, bite-size. There weren't a lot of roads, and they all seemed to end up at the same place.

Decades later, when I started writing fiction, I used Cullman as a backdrop for where I set my stories. More than a backdrop, it was a template. I used to think of setting as the least important element of a story, but that was because, in the beginning, so many of my stories happened in living rooms and kitchens. But when I became more adept at moving my characters around, I needed a place for them to move around in, and Cullman became that place. I never mentioned the town by name, but *Big Fish* and *The Watermelon King*, my third novel, take place in Cullman, and so many stories besides.

What I would do is this: I'd begin with the town, its layout, stores and homes and basic architecture. But it would be empty of life. Not a soul roamed its streets. And in each story I'd bring in a whole crop of new characters, freshly minted made-up people to love and hate on the same old streets, live in the same houses, shop at the same stores, and when the story or novel was finished, those folks would be asked to leave. The town would be evacuated. The homes and buildings would remain, but nothing else. A ghost town. My process here is akin to a *Twilight Zone* episode.

Anyway, the reason I bring up Cullman is to say, it's actually the exact opposite of the Spectre scenario. Cullman is a real place I turned into a story.

There are so many ways the imagined story in the novel *Big Fish* found a life in a world outside its pages, and so many of them concern my father.

This tale concerns Specter as well.

When Edward Bloom buys Specter, he meets a woman there named Jenny Hill, and they have an affair. Since he owns the town, he puts her up in one of his houses, and when he leaves his home and his family on business trips, he goes to Specter and stays with her. This goes on for a bit, but, eventually, Edward stops going to Specter. The woman he loved there, and who loved him, is left all alone with a broken heart.

"People go by the house at night and they swear they can see faint yellow lights at the window, two of them, her eyes, glowing in her head… In a matter of days the vines grow from one side of the house to the other, finally covering it over until it's hard to know there is a house there at all."

In due course a swamp appears and surrounds the house; no one can even reach the front door—even Edward, who goes back and tries. "He can no longer have her," his son, William, writes, "and that is why he is so sad and tired when he comes home, and why he has so little to say."

This chapter was written in 1996. In 1997, my father died. By then he and my mother had been long divorced, and he had remarried. He had also become the big fish he always wanted to be. By any estimation, he was a great success. He owned houses all over the world.

But in going through his papers, we discovered he owned another house, a house we didn't know he had—a house no one knew he had. It was in Birmingham, not far from where I grew up. Not a modest house either: The documentation we saw that day in the lawyer's office valued the property at over $300,000. This was over 20 years ago. Now it must be worth millions.

What we eventually came to understand is that a woman lived in the house—a woman who was my father's mistress. It turned out I'd met her a couple of times, because she was his housecleaner. That's how they met, when she was hired to clean his condominium. Sometimes when I came into town and stayed at my father's place she'd come over and clean. She was pleasant and pretty, and not in the age group you might think—close enough to my father's age to be respectable. But I had no idea they were together, no one did, and that they'd been together for some time. He'd bought this house for her, and when he was in Birmingham, which was about half the time, this is where he lived. He had his calls forwarded from his condominium, and if you called him and she answered, she would say hi, yes, she was there, at his condo, cleaning. My father was close to her children and grandchildren; they stayed there sometimes. He had more than another woman in that house: He had another family.

When all this was discovered, the woman was asked to leave, and she did. I saw her at my father's service, but this was before we knew about the house. I've never seen her again. I have no idea what happened to her, or even if she's still alive.


Living not far from Spectre, and taking care of it as best they can, are Lynn and Bobby Bright. Lynn is a retired judge; Bobby was mayor of Montgomery, and now he's running for Congress. The town of Spectre—one long street with homes and stores on either side, and a church at the end of the lane, not much more than an acre all told—is on Jackson Lake Island, a 60-acre island in the middle of the Alabama River, a place people go to kayak, fish and camp—and to see what's left of the townlet portrayed in the movie, to see the wire where Jenny Hill tied the laces of Edward Bloom's shoes together and slung them up there, looping them over it on her first try.

That wire is still there, and people still loop their shoes over it. Especially couples who come there to get married. Goats live inside the church now—beyond the vestibule, it's just dirt—but weddings are held in front of it, and afterward the couple will tie the laces of their shoes together and toss them up until they get hung on the wire. "We have to clear the line every couple of months, it gets so full of shoes," Lynn told me. She loves it that people come here to do that. "We could have a used-shoe store here."

> "IN A MATTER OF DAYS THE VINES GROW FROM ONE SIDE OF THE HOUSE TO THE OTHER, FINALLY COVERING IT OVER UNTIL IT'S HARD TO KNOW THERE IS A HOUSE THERE AT ALL."

Lynn isn't sure how many people come to Jackson Lake Island to see Spectre. The entrance fee is $3, but during the week it's on the honor system; other than on Saturday and Sunday, no one is at the gate. "I'll say a hundred," she says. "At least a 100 people a week. And they come from all over the world. France, Lithuania.

A man came here with a tattoo of the fish from the movie. It covered the top part of his entire back. It was a foot and a half long at least. Kids get their graduation photos here. Just all kinds of things."

For a few years after the movie, no one, including the Brights, paid much attention to Spectre. The goats took over the entire place; trees grew up inside the houses. But in 2010, Roadside America and BuzzFeed ran stories about the town's ghostly existence, and all that changed. Spectre got a second life. Or maybe a third.

It's not easy to maintain a small village on an island in the Alabama River, and Lynn doesn't know how long it's going to hold up. We talked about having a fundraiser for it. I could come down and read from a part from the book that I made up, about the town that I made up, in the town that was made up to be that town. Which is not weird at all.

I'm not sure what I think about all this. I've never been comfortable, or particularly adept, at articulating abstractions, writing about our meta lives. I approach something like this the way I do the flourishes of amazement we encounter, from time to time, in the world: with wonder, just wonder, that such a thing could actually happen.

It should come as no wonder, though, by now, that everything bleeds into everything else.

*The New York Times* sent a reporter down to Chapel Hill in January 2004, a month after the movie was released, to talk to me about my father. My father was the inspiration for the father in the book, although I don't think they—my actual father and the character based on him—would have recognized each other if somehow they'd been able to meet. Still, without the father I had I never would have been able to write the book I did, and no movie would have been made. This is why a writer named Dinitia Smith flew all the way down to Chapel Hill to talk to me.

I talked too much. I knew it even then, even as I was talking too much. But I couldn't stop. I told her more than she ever wanted to know about my father, about my father and me. How charming he was but how "when he came into the room, he wanted you to know it." I told her he drank too much, bullied his children sometimes and was something of a storyteller him-

self—but in the interview I called him a liar. I was trying to make a distinction: A storyteller tells stories for the benefit of others; a liar tells stories to benefit himself.

I didn't think I had been callous; there was nothing I said that wasn't true. And yet he was a good man who did great things. I don't think that came through in the piece, though, and it was my fault it didn't.

One of the saddest stories he told about himself, and I mentioned this in the interview, was toward the end of his life. By that time he had become the big fish he'd always wanted to be, with his own plane and houses all over the world. He had remarried, to a lovely woman who seemed to know everybody in the art, literary and political world. Some pretty fancy people with pretty fancy pedigrees.

My father, a country boy from the hills of Alabama, started wearing an ascot.

My father, who had attended one semester of college at Auburn University, told his new friends that he'd gone to Yale. And he had. But not *that* Yale.

Yale Cooking School.

This is the saddest story, I think. Not that he went to Yale Cooking School, but that he couldn't tell his new group of friends that he did.

The article in the *Times* was published on January 31, 2004.

On February 7, *The New York Times* published a letter from my step-mother, his widow, responding to the article. She wrote that the "man described is unknown to me, his widow. Dan was neither a cheat, a liar, braggart or bully. He was honest, self-deprecating, generous and fair."

At least one other letter was sent to the *Times*, not just protesting the tenor of the piece but disqualifying me, as his son, from having an accurate, objective perception of who my father was.

*He did go to Yale! they said. He didn't cheat or lie! He loved wearing ascots!*

My father was many things, as we all are. He could be very generous, and there were a number of times he was to me. But I was too honest in that interview. No one needed to know that stuff about my father. And that's why his widow snuck in behind me and, without even a note to me about it, sent that letter into the *Times*. She was taking care of his story. She was feathering the myth. She was doing in real life what I was doing in real fiction. Making things up.

All this happened in 2004, seven years after he died, and seven years after we all found out about the other family.

In 2014, his widow and I forgave each other for everything we did or might have done, via post. But we haven't spoken to each other in 14 years.


Cullman was the small pond my father left to follow his watery dreams. But in a twist, all of my dreams are born in Cullman's streets. The Southern town he loved but which was not enough for him has turned out to be more than enough for me. I've lived in North Carolina for almost 40 years, but no fiction of mine has found a place here. Almost all of them take place in two, three square-mile patches of land, one in Birmingham and the other in Cullman. Specter is also Ashland is also Cullman is also Spectre is also Roam and also any number of nameless towns my ragtag group of sketchy characters might pass through, stop over in, swing by. Any place that is a place: It's somewhere near the middle of Alabama.

In 1978, I spent a summer on Smith Lake, a man-made lake not far from Cullman. We had a rickety old cabin there. I went there to write. I brought my Brother typewriter, an AM/FM radio, gin, tonic and my dog, Orsin, a bulldog. He sat in his own chair at the table, slept in the bed at my feet. I also brought two books: the Modern Library edition of *Ulysses* and a book that explained *Ulysses*, chapter by chapter. I drank gin and smoked cigarettes and watched the lake level get lower and lower every day. A hot, rainless summer, and by the end of it the dock was resting on the rocky shore, planks of pointless plywood. But I didn't write. A couple of times a week I'd go into town for lunch, dinner with my Aunt Sis or drive just over the county line to the closest wet county. But I didn't write.

It wasn't that I didn't try. I tried to write. Every morning I tried, facing the Brother like a matador faces an oncoming bull, fingers resting on the keys, waiting for one of the fingers to press one of the keys. To tap out a letter that might turn into a word, just a single word that might lead me get to another, that eventually, over time, might lead to one complete sentence.

It was a long, sad summer. Waiting for something to happen

stretches time like a rubber band; every moment I felt like I was going to snap. I don't know what I thought was going to happen, but it didn't. By the end of that summer I had written ten pages of words, but no story. Just words. Not even the onionskin paper I had chosen to type on helped. All that became clear to me is that I wasn't going to be a writer. If I couldn't write under the most ideal circumstances, alone with a dog on a lake, I was certain I wouldn't be able to write over the course of time through a real life.

What didn't happen then happened 20 years later: I wrote a book. I wrote a book that never could have been written had I not spent that summer on Smith Lake not writing the book I had wanted to. Inspiration is an emotional memory set to an internal timer over which we have no control. We just have to be ready for it when it goes off.

This is when mine went off.

One more thing. I'd almost forgotten this.

I'd written five of what I'll call "practice novels" before the lucky one that was finally published, *Big Fish*. I'd shown my father a couple of the early ones, and he didn't think much of them. I'd taken it personally at the time, but, to his credit, there wasn't much to think of them, except that they weren't very good.

*Big Fish* is about a father and a son, and the father is dying, and finally does die, at the end of it. But as I was writing this, killing the fictional father off day after day, my real father was fine. He was traveling around the world, relaxing on the vast acreage he'd bought on the Eastern Shore.

I think you can see where this is going.

We didn't talk much in those days, not for any real reason. We were just doing our own things. So when he called it was a surprise, and I knew there had to be a reason for it. There was. He told me he was going to be in the hospital for a couple of days. Open-heart surgery. Quadruple bypass. "It's nothing, really," he said. "They've got these things down. It's almost a drive-through operation these days."

He was funny.

Of course, he died.

Of course he did.

How much power do words have? Maybe not so much. But on the other hand, you can't cast magic spells without them: It's how a man becomes a newt.

So I disagree. Words are powerful things. But can a story change or predict the future? The answer to that is: obviously. *Big Fish* the book didn't kill my father, any more than the movie *Big Fish* killed Spalding Gray, who threw himself into the Hudson River after watching it. But I do believe that an imagined world can create real space in the real one, and in the mind and heart of a reader, and in this way change occurs. It's a reason we tell stories at all. Blue Eye, Fairhope, Smoke Rise, Burnt Corn, Cullman, Spectre. One's no more real than the other.

---

**DANIEL WALLACE** is the author of seven novels, including *Big Fish, Ray in Reverse, The Watermelon King* and most recently *Extraordinary Adventures. Big Fish* was made into a motion picture of the same name by Tim Burton in 2003. Wallace lives in Chapel Hill, North Carolina, and teaches creative writing at UNC.

# "GRACE"

*By Jake Adam York*

*Because my grandmother made me*
*the breakfast her mother made her,*
*when I crack the eggs, pat the butter*
*on the toast, and remember the bacon*
*to cast iron, to fork, to plate, to tongue,*
*my great grandmother moves my hands*
*to whisk, to spatula, to biscuit ring,*
*and I move her hands too, making*
*her mess, so the syllable of batter*
*I'll find tomorrow beneath the fridge*
*and the strew of salt and oil are all*
*memorials, like the pan-fried chicken*
*that whistles in the grease in the voice*
*of my best friend's grandmother*
*like a midnight mockingbird,*
*and the smoke from the grill*
*is the smell of my father coming home*
*from the furnace and the tang*
*of vinegar and char is the smell*
*of Birmingham, the smell*
*of coming home, of history, redolent*
*as the salt of black-and-white film*
*when I unwrap the sandwich*
*from the wax-paper the wax-paper*
*crackling like the cold grass*
*along the Selma to Montgomery road,*
*like the foil that held*
*Medgar's last meal, a square of tin*
*that is just the ghost of that barbecue*
*I can imagine to my tongue*

*when I stand at the pit with my brother*
*and think of all the hands and mouths*
*and breaths of air that sharpened*
*this flavor and handed it down to us,*
*I feel all those hands inside*
*my hands when it's time to spread*
*the table linen or lift a coffin rail*
*and when the smoke billows from the pit*
*I think of my uncle, I think of my uncle*
*rising, not falling, when I raise*
*the buttermilk and the cornmeal to the light*
*before giving them to the skillet*
*and sometimes I say the recipe*
*to the air and sometimes I say his name*
*or her name or her name*
*and sometimes I just set the table*
*because meals are memorials*
*that teach us how to move,*
*history moves in us as we raise*
*our voices and then our glasses*
*to pour a little out for those*
*who poured out everything for us,*
*we pour ourselves for them,*
*so they can eat again.*

---

**JAKE ADAM YORK** was a poet. Born in West Palm Beach, Florida, and raised in Gadsden, Alabama, he published three books of poetry: *Murder Ballads*, *A Murmuration of Starlings* and *Persons Unknown*. A fourth, *Abide*, was published after his death, in 2012.

# INDEX

A state-by-state catalog of contact information for recommended restaurants and bars, hotels and inns, shops, outfitters, museums, service providers and more

# INDEX

16 Bud and Alley's, Seaside
1236 East County Road
30-A
budandalleys.com

71 Indian Pass Raw Bar,
Port St. Joe
8391 Hwy C-30A
indianpassrawbar.com

72 Lazy Flamingo,
Sanibel
1036 Periwinkle Way
lazyflamingo.com

70 The Red Bar,
Grayton Beach
70 Hotz Ave
theredbar.com

16 Roy's, Steinhatchee
100 1st Ave SW
roys-restaurant.com
......................

ACTIVITY

73 Bahia Honda State
Park, Big Pine Key
36850 Overseas Hwy
bahiahondapark.com

72 Bailey-Matthews
National Shell Museum,
Sanibel
3075 Sanibel Captiva Rd
shellmuseum.org

72 Chassahowitzka
Springs, Homosassa
8600 W Miss Maggie Dr

72 Ginnie Springs,
High Springs
7300 Ginnie Springs Rd
ginniespringsoutdoors.com

16 Joseph's Cottage,
Port St. Joe
403 Reid Ave
josephscottage.com

45 Kingsley Plantation,
Jacksonville
11676 Palmetto Ave

72 Three Sisters Springs,
Crystal River
601 Three Sisters Springs Tr
threesisterspringsvisitor.org

16 Weeki Wachee Springs
State Park, Spring Hill
6131 Commercial Way
weekiwachee.com

## GEORGIA

12 The Cloister,
Sea Island
100 Cloister Drive
seaisland.com

24 The Gastonian,
Savannah
220 E Gaston St
gastonian.com

75 Greyfield Inn,
Cumberland Island
4 N 2nd St
greyfieldinn.com

12 Hike Inn, Dawsonville
280 Amicalola Falls
State Park Rd
hike-inn.com

12 Hotel Clermont,
Atlanta
789 Ponce de Leon Ave NE
hotelclermont.com
......................

FOOD & DRINK

24, 75 Back in the Day
Bakery, Savannah
2403 Bull St
backinthedaybakery.com

48 Busy Bee Cafe, Atlanta
810 M.L. King Jr Dr SW
thebusybeecafe.com

69 Flora-Bama,
Orange Beach
17401 Perdido Key Dr
florabama.com

16 Fresh Air Barbecue,
Jackson
1164 Hwy 42 S
freshairbarbecue.com

24 The Grey, Savannah
109 Martin Luther
King Jr. Blvd
thegreyrestaurant.com

48 Mary Mac's Tea
Room, Atlanta
224 Ponce De Leon
Ave NE
marymacs.com

9 Miller Union, Atlanta
999 Brady Ave NW
millerunion.com

61 Pho Dai Loi #2,
Atlanta
4186 Buford Hwy NE
404-633-2111

61 El Rey del Taco,
Doraville
5288 Buford Hwy NE
elreydeltacoatl.com

75 Speed's Kitchen,
Townsend
1191 Speeds Kitchen Rd NE
912-832-4763

16 Ticonderoga Club,
Atlanta
99 Krog St NE
ticonderogaclub.com

48 Weaver D's, Athens
1016 E Broad St
weaverds.com

61 Yet Tuh, Doraville
3042 Oakcliff Rd
770-454-9292
......................

ACTIVITY

24 Forsyth Park,
Savannah
Drayton St & Gaston St

45 Fort Frederica
National Monument, St.
Simons Island
6515 Frederica Rd

45 Hog Hammock ferry,
Sapelo Island
sapelonerr.org/
visit-sapelo-island

45 McIntosh Sugar Mill
Park, St. Mary's
Charlie Smith Sr Hwy

16 Savannah Bee
Company
Various locations
savannahbee.com

24 SCAD Museum of
Art, Savannah
601 Turner Blvd
scadmoa.org

92 Sid and Ann
Mashburn, Atlanta
1198 Howell Mill Rd
sidmashburn.com,
annmashburn.com

66 Central Grocery,
New Orleans
923 Decatur St
*centralgrocery.com*

66 Commander's Palace,
New Orleans
1403 Washington Ave
*commanderspalace.com*

17, 66 Galatoire's,
New Orleans
209 Bourbon St
*galatoires.com*

66 Hansen's,
New Orleans
4801 Tchoupitoulas St
*snobliz.com*

23 Johnson's
Boucanière, Lafayette
1111 St John St
*johnsonsboucaniere.com*

23 Laura's II,
Lafayette
1904 W University Ave
337-593-8006

66 Parkway Bakery &
Tavern, New Orleans
538 Hagan Ave
*parkwaypoorboys.com*

66 Pascal's Manale,
New Orleans
1838 Napoleon Ave
*pascalsmanale.com*

52 Revel Cafe & Bar,
New Orleans
133 N Carrollton Ave
*revelcafeandbar.com*

65 Whiskey River
Landing, Henderson
365 Henderson
Levee Rd
*whiskeyriverla.com*
..........................

ACTIVITY

96 Preservation Hall,
New Orleans
726 St Peter St
*preservationhall.com*

65 Savoy Music Center,
Eunice
4413 US-190 E
*savoymusiccenter.com*

## MISSISSIPPI

LODGING

77 Alluvian Hotel,
Greenwood
318 Howard St
*thealluvian.com*
..........................

FOOD & DRINK

77 Big Apple Inn, Jackson
509 N Farish St
601-354-9371

48 Bully's Restaurant,
Jackson
3118 Livingston Rd
601-362-0484

77 Doe's Eat Place,
Greenville
502 Nelson St
*doeseatplace.com*

77, 113 Lusco's,
Greenwood
722 Carrollton Ave
*luscos.net*

17 Taylor Grocery,
Taylor
4 1st St
*taylorgrocery.com*
..........................

ACTIVITY

77 Highway 61 Blues
Museum, Leland
307 North Broad St
*highway61blues.com*

64 Lemuria Books, Jackson
4465 N Hwy 55
*lemuriabooks.com*

77 Mississippi Civil
Rights Museum, Jackson
222 North St
*mcrm.mdah.ms.gov*

69 Ohr-O'Keefe
Museum of Art, Biloxi
386 Beach Blvd
*georgeohr.org*

77 Red's Lounge,
Clarksdale
398 Sunflower Ave

69 Shearwater Pottery,
Ocean Springs
102 Shearwater Dr
*shearwaterpottery.com*

64 Square Books,
Oxford
160 Courthouse Sq
*squarebooks.com*

64 Turnrow Books,
Greenwood
304 Howard St
*turnrowbooks.com*

69 Walter Anderson
Museum of Art,
Ocean Springs
510 Washington Ave
*walteranderson
museum.org*
..........................

## NORTH
## CAROLINA

LODGING

79 The Grove Park Inn,
Asheville
290 Macon Ave
*omnihotels.com/hotels/
asheville-grove-park*

12 High Hampton
Resort, Cashiers
1525 Hwy 107 S
*highhamptonresort.com*

25 Sanderling Resort,
Duck
1461 Duck Rd
*sanderling-resort.com*
..........................

FOOD & DRINK

59 Baby Scratch, Durham
1022 Chapel Hill Rd
*piefantasy.com*

25 The Backstreet Pub,
Beaufort
124 Middle Ln
252-781-7108

25 Beaufort Grocery,
Beaufort
117 Queen St
*beaufortgrocery.com*

79 Burial Beer Co.,
Asheville
40 Collier Ave
*burialbeer.com*

79 Buxton Hall, Asheville
32 Banks Ave
*buxtonhall.com*